WILLIAM
WILBERFORCE

WILLIAM
WILBERFORCE

GREATEST WORKS

Bridge-Logos
Alachua, FL 32615 USA

Bridge-Logos

Alachua, FL 32615 USA

Wilberforce: Greatest Works
by William Wilberforce

Printed in the United States of America.

Library of Congress Catalog Card Number: 2007921858
International Standard Book Number: 978-0-88270-370-1

Scripture quotations are from the *King James Version* of the Bible.

G.163.317.B.m802.35450

CONTENTS

Foreword vii

Introduction xi

Part 1
ABOUT THE MAN AND HIS WORKS

1   The Shrimp Who Became a Whale 1

   Gallery 27

2   The Clapham Group: They Set Out to Change
   Their World 33

Part 2
EXCERPTS FROM A PRACTICAL VIEW OF THE PREVAILING RELIGIOUS SYSTEM OF PROFESSED CHRISTIANS IN THE HIGHER AND MIDDLE CLASSES, CONTRASTED WITH REAL CHRISTIANITY

3   Inadequate Conceptions of the Importance of
   Christianity 43

4   Corruption of Human Nature 53

5   Chief Defects of the Religious System / the Use of
   Passions in Religion 75

6   On the Excellence of Christianity 115

Part 3

TRIBUTES TO WILLIAM WILBERFORCE

7   Epistle to William Wilberforce, Esq. on the Rejection
    of the Bill for Abolishing the Slave Trade 125

8   Newspaper Accounts of Wilberforce's Funeral 131

9   William Cowper's Poems 141

10 Spirit of the Age: A Contemporary Evaluates
    Wilberforce 145

11 Tribute to William Wilberforce by William Jay ... 151

12 Tribute to William Wilberforce on the Plaque in
    Westminster Abbey Where He Is Buried 169

13 Wilberforce's Text 175

Bibliography 185

Index 187

FOREWORD

Ye are the salt of the earth. ...Ye are the light of the world. ... Let your light so shine before men, that they may see your good works and glorify your Father which is in heaven (Matthew 5:13-16).

It almost seems as if Jesus was describing William Wilberforce by way of the salt and light metaphors He used in His Sermon on the Mount, for Wilberforce's influence on Western society's laws and morals has never been surpassed by any other modern Christian, and his profound influence lives on today.

This uniquely committed man brought light into a world that was hideously darkened by the meanness and corruption of slavery. The light he shone dispelled the darkness of slavery in his own time in the British Isles, and it continued to penetrate the darkness after his death, when President Abraham Lincoln signed the Emancipation Proclamation, freeing the slaves in America, as well.

Though small in stature, William Wilberforce was a true giant and a valiant champion. His Christian leadership in areas of morality, integrity, and righteousness continues to effect changes both in the Church and society today. He was ever circumspect about walking the Christian walk in front of others and ever vigilant about sharing the Gospel of Jesus Christ without any shame or pretense.

He articulated the Christian message in perceptive and practical ways. That's one of the reasons why we've included the important excerpts from his influential classic, *A Practical View of the Prevailing Religious System of Professed Christians in the Higher and Middle Classes, Contrasted With Real Christianity,* in this book. It is a message that needs to be heard by Christians today, for its contrasts are as relevant now as they were in the 1800s.

In the sections of his book, which we have sensitively revised and updated, Wilberforce shows how nominal Christians differ from "real Christians," and he does so by painting verbal pictures that are lucid, insightful, and profound. In addition, he explicates the Scriptures with authority and conviction and calls believers to a deeper walk with the Lord.

In our revision of his text we have added Scripture references, deleted obscure examples, and slightly revised some of the words and sentences he used in order to give them a more modern appeal, while always being careful to retain the author's original style and intent. As a result, Wilberforce's message comes through loudly and clearly.

Nearly two centuries have passed since Wilberforce wrote his book, and so certain subtle changes in syntax and semantics had to be addressed, so that the modern reader would be able to appreciate the depth of this man's knowledge and commitment. For the most part, however, we've retained his original words. This allows the reader to experience the flavor of the times in which it was written, thereby providing new perspectives on the timeless message of the Gospel.

This is the 200th anniversary of the passage by the British Parliament of the Abolition of Slavery Act, which represents the culmination of Wilberforce's work. We are pleased to commemorate this anniversary with a book that you will find to be informative, inspirational, and very moving. It contains a vital message that needs to be read by people today, because it provides both light and salt to a world that still struggles with spiritual darkness.

Lloyd B. Hildebrand
Senior Editor
Bridge-Logos Publishers

INTRODUCTION

William Wilberforce (August 24, 1759–July 29, 1833) was a statesman, philanthropist, author and leader of England in the abolition of the slave trade. This last role is perhaps what he is best known for, which has assured him a prominent place in history. Wilberforce, however, was much more than this.

It needs to be noted that throughout his illustrious career, Wilberforce suffered many physical ailments. He had weak eyesight; he walked like a hunchback and had many other things that would have excused him from the public arena. Despite all the obstacles, both physical and political, nothing deterred him from his goal as he envisioned it.

His physical appearance belied the strength of character and commitment he possessed. Someone once described him as a "shrimp," and from his physical appearance, one could rapidly come to that conclusion. Although it might have been a weakness, it turned out to be a great strength for him and the many battles he fought. His opponents, particularly in the political arena, underestimated the strength and ability of this man. Too often, they cast him aside only to regret it in the end. Consequently, he succeeded where other people might have succumbed to failure.

As you read this book, pay particular attention to chapter three, "*The Epistle to William Wilberforce,*" by Anna Laetitia

Barbauld (1743–1825). It was written after the *Rejection of the Bill for Abolishing the Slave Trade* in the British Parliament. This was a great defeat for William Wilberforce. Any lesser man would have quit right here. In spite of defeat after defeat, public humiliation and desertion by some of his friends, Wilberforce fought on, giving no room or allowances for defeat.

During this time, he suffered great personal humiliation. More times than not, while walking down the street somebody would come up and spit in his face. Many people hated him and prophesied his demise. Nevertheless, year after year, he only gained strength and support for his causes.

The last part of Barbauld's poem sounds a mighty woeful, defeating note:

> "Succeeding times your struggles, and their fate,
> With mingled shame and triumph shall relate,
> While faithful History, in her various page,
> Marking the features of this motley age,
> To shed a glory, and to fix a stain,
> Tells how you strove, and that you strove in vain."

From her point of view, Wilberforce "strove in vain."

History has forgotten her; however, 200 years later we are still celebrating the great achievement of William Wilberforce. History vindicates his efforts and that he did not strive in vain, but his mighty, tireless work in this one aspect has paid rich dividends. All his opponents have fallen into obscurity while he remains a solitary figure of success particularly in the area of abolishing the slave trade.

In his fight against slavery, Wilberforce was not alone. Certainly, throughout the years, many of his friends deserted him, but there were some who stood shoulder to shoulder with him in this great endeavor. I think the second chapter on The Clapham Group, is quite revealing. Although these names have long faded into oblivion, their encouragement and support of Wilberforce during his darkest hours enabled him to carry on. They provided him the moral and spiritual support he needed to go into the lion's den. Like Daniel before him, Wilberforce faced the lion in his den and absolutely defeated him to roar no more.

Wilberforce was a writer, politician par excellence and reformer of his generation. But the most significant thing about Wilberforce was his conversion to Christianity. That was the turning point, not only in his life, but also in the life of a nation and generation.

It is interesting to note that Wilberforce started his political career as a non-believer. He came from a well-stationed family with a successful business. Following his college career, he turned his back on the family business and surprised everybody by entering the political arena. Such a one as William Wilberforce did not seem a likely candidate for any political office. Yet, he made quite a mark upon the political life in Great Britain. He was the youngest man who ever won the seat in the Ministry of Parliament.

It was only after some talks with John Newton and John Wesley that his life took on a dramatic change. Before his conversion, he was simply out for himself and all that he could achieve in order to advance selfish interests. Following his conversion, he had a very different outlook on life. In fact, he thought about giving up politics and perhaps pursuing some other line of work more conducive to his Christian convictions.

He was finally convinced he could best serve Christ through a political career. And the world is grateful that he did. In a day and age when politics seems like a dirty game, a new generation of young people needs to be challenged by the life of William Wilberforce.

The bits and pieces collected in this book only suggest the importance and significance of William Wilberforce in his generation. From a physical standpoint, Wilberforce had the appearance of being weak and insignificant. However, there was a passion burning in his heart that had been ignited by God. The gross injustices of his generation fanned the flames into a full moral conflagration that set the world on fire.

It seems incredible that an entire society embraced slavery as though it was normal and proper. It took one man to challenge the ethical protocol of slavery and make not only a nation but also the world look at slavery for the evil it was. I would recommend a careful reading of his famous abolition speech found in Chapter nine. Of course, the language is over 200 years old, but the sentiment and passion of his beating heart is as fresh today as ever. Drink deeply of his enthusiasm and allow it to adorn your heart for the contemporary issues that need the same strength of commitment.

Not only did Wilberforce lend his indomitable spirit to the abolition of slavery but he also challenged the decay of the Christianity of his time. He began to notice a serious decline and decay of Christianity in his time. He knew how much Christianity had changed his heart and paved the way for brilliant career in politics. His concern was that Great Britain was losing her spiritual and moral moorings. Out of that concern, he wrote a book.

When he published his book, *A Practical View of Christianity,* his publisher did not see much of a market for such a book. I think the publisher only printed 500 copies initially, and was almost reluctant to do that. However, God surprised both author and publisher with a tremendous sale of this book in Great Britain as well as America. It also had a great impact on the culture of his day.

To understand his impact upon his generation one has only to read the newspaper accounts found in this book. The whole world mourned his death. William's life emphasizes the truth that when God gets a hold of a person's life great things can ensue. Read Wilberforce and get to understand his passion. Meditate upon his work in ministry and allow God to surge up within you a passion for the times in which we live. The world has need of another William Wilberforce to step forward with incomparable faith in God and a tireless spirit of service despite personal obstacles.

Part 1

ABOUT THE MAN
AND HIS WORKS

Chapter One

WILLIAM WILBERFORCE:
THE SHRIMP WHO BECAME A WHALE

William Wilberforce was one of the greatest social reformers in British history, if not all history. The dynamic of his tireless work was the belief that every man and woman is made in the image of God and therefore of infinite worth. Although this might seem trite today, in Wilberforce's day it was not commonly held. This zeal drove him to spend over 30 years, most of his political career, tirelessly campaigning to end slavery.

No Englishman ever accomplished more to challenge the conscience of the British people, to elevate and ennoble British life. In his time, Christianity suffered a decline. Wilberforce devoted much time and energy to attack this crisis. His publication of *A Practical View of the Prevailing Religious System ... Contrasted with Real Christianity* (1797) was a noble attempt to do this. Nobody was more surprised than Wilberforce on the wide sale of this book. Originally, the publisher only printed 500 copies. Before long, they realized that more had to be printed and the book went through many editions during Wilberforce's lifetime.

He was said to be "the wittiest man in England, and the most religious" (Madame de Stael), and one who possessed

1

"the greatest natural eloquence of all the men I ever met" (William Pitt). When he spoke, another quipped, "The shrimp became a whale" (James Boswell). Historian G. M. Trevelyan called this "shrimp" the primary human agent for "one of the turning events in the history of the world."

It is hard to imagine this man, with the gentle grin and the small, twisted body could move the world in a new direction. Yet William Wilberforce did. He was the "shrimp that became a whale" by the grace and determination of God.

Weak and painful eyes, a stomach prone to colitis and a body that for many years had to be held upright by a crude metal frame, blighted Wilberforce's health. In his late 20s, he already wrote from his sickbed, "[I] am still a close prisoner, wholly unequal even to such a little business as I am now engaged in: add to which my eyes are so bad that I can scarce see how to direct my pen."

His gloomy doctor reported, "That little fellow, with his calico guts, cannot possibly survive a twelve-month."

He did, though in the process he became dependent on small doses of opium, the nearest thing to an effective painkiller and treatment for colitis known at the time. Wilberforce was aware of opium's dangers and was not easily persuaded to take it. After taking it for some time, he noticed that omitting his nighttime dose caused sickness, sweating, and sneezing in the morning. Opium's hallucinatory powers terrified him, and the depressions it caused virtually crippled him at times.

His notebooks contain anguished prayers: "I fly to thee for succor and support, O Lord, let it come speedily. ... I am in great troubles insurmountable by me. ... Look upon me, O Lord, with compassion and mercy, and restore me to rest, quietness and comfort in the world, or in another by removing me hence into a state of happiness." In his later years, he showed the long-term effects of opium use, particularly listlessness and amnesia.

Born on August 24, 1759, the third child of Robert and Elizabeth Wilberforce grew up surrounded by wealth. The Wilberforces had settled in Hull, England, at the beginning of the 1700s and made their wealth in the booming Baltic trade. The family consisted of four children in all, three girls and William. He was a small and feeble child, with weak eyes, but compensated with a strong and great spirit defying his frail body. Thoughtful far beyond his years for others, affectionate, gentle, clever, quick and active, possessing a melodious voice, his was a very attractive personality. He began his education at seven years of age and his elocution was so remarkably good, he was frequently set on a table and made to read aloud as an example to the other boys.

When Wilberforce was nine, his father died, and he was sent to live with his uncle, William Wilberforce, at Wimbledon, and St. James Place. There he went to school in Putney, for two years. At this time, George Whitefield was preaching in London, and his aunt's admiration of his teaching soon had its effect on the nephew.

When Wilberforce's mother caught wind of this, she, fearing the "poison" of Methodism might infect her son, brought him back to Hull and enrolled him at Pockington near York. His education as a gentleman continued among the prevailing "aristocracy." He learned to play cards and sing and developed his gift of witty repartee. At parties, he was always the center of attention.

His mother did everything possible to clear his mind of any piety or seriousness, and was quite successful. Idleness and love of pleasure were encouraged, and he excelled in it all.

COLLEGE

In 1776 at seventeen, he went to St. John's College, Cambridge. With plenty of money at his disposal, for his grandfather and uncle had both left him a fortune, he entered upon his university career under what many could consider very favorable conditions. Here he was flattered, and idleness was encouraged. People advised him, "Why should a man of your fortune trouble himself with fagging?" And he didn't.

Later Wilberforce wrote, "I was naturally a high-spirited boy and fiery. They [his friends] pushed me forward and made me talk a great deal and made me very vain." His natural abilities and gifts in this area made him popular and with great diligence, he made himself available at all parties.

"As much pains were taken to make me idle as were ever taken to make anyone studious," he later complained. Although he possessed enormous intellectual aspirations, they too easily succumbed to his passion for socializing. A neighbor, Thomas Gisborne, later recalled, "When he [Wilberforce] returned late in the evening to his rooms, he would summon me to join him.... He was so winning and amusing that I often sat up half the night with him, much to the detriment of my attendance at lectures the next day."

Wilberforce graduated from St. John's College, Cambridge the same year as the hardworking William Pitt (future Prime Minister). Their friendship grew throughout 1779 and together they watched Parliament from the gallery and dreamed of political careers. Those "dreams" were fulfilled beyond their wildest expectations and later they would join forces in some of the greatest political challenges of their time.

A POLITICAL CAREER

After graduation, Wilberforce quickly renounced the vast business interests, which he inherited from father and grandfather, and determined to enter public life. The life of the politician seemed quite attractive to him. At least, it seemed an easy way to earn a living as well as the respect of people. At this point, there were no thoughts of reformation in any regard clouding his thinking.

In the summer of 1780, the ambitious Wilberforce stood for election as a Member of Parliament (MP) for Hull. He was only 21, and one of his opponents had powerful supporters. His chances of winning were slim. Surprising everyone, Wilberforce relying on his charm, energy, tact and powers of persuasion, secured as many votes as his opponents combined. He won a great victory and was to remain a Member of Parliament, for various constituencies, for another 45 years.

"The first years I was in Parliament," he later wrote, "I did nothing—nothing that is to any purpose. My own distinction was my darling object."

As a Member of Parliament, he became a frequent visitor of the exclusive clubs of St. James and acquired a reputation as a songster and wit but most regarded him as "careless and inaccurate in method." His fertile mind flitted from topic to topic and his early speeches, though eloquent, lacked focus and passion.

Shortly afterwards Wilberforce went to London, where he was warmly welcomed, and, as he says, "at once immersed in politics and fashion." He was a member of five clubs, and very soon, he was gambling. On one occasion, he won a large sum of money from someone who could not afford it. This so greatly pained him, that he was absolutely cured of gambling from that time. Immensely popular, his uncommonly good singing called forth the admiration of the Prince of Wales, who, at one of the Devonshire House Soirees, declared he would come at anytime to hear him.

When Wilberforce entered Parliament, the ministry of Lord Norm had been in power for ten years, serving virtually as a mere cloak for the direction of public affairs by King George III. The times were difficult for Great Britain. Rebellion had been instigated in the American colonies, then combated stubbornly and inefficiently; the country had been involved in war with Holland and France; public expenditures had risen alarmingly.

One historian writes, "On the other hand, certain of the laws against the Roman Catholics had been repealed, and Give had founded the English dominion in India, while Warren Hastings was following brilliantly in his footsteps. Though professedly opposed to the North ministry, at first Wilberforce voted with it on certain secondary measures. In 1782 William Pitt came into power, and thenceforth, with but brief intervals, stood at the head of affairs until his death in 1806. Pitt and Wilberforce were contemporaries at Cambridge, they became friendly during the parliamentary election of 1780 and soon after, they became close and intimate friends. In general, Wilberforce supported heartily the liberal and reformatory policy of the minister, especially during the pre-Revolutionary period. Yet he was never a blind partisan, and at times worked and voted against his friend— notably, he opposed English participation in the war with France in 1793 and succeeding years, and in 1805 supported the impeachment of Lord Melville "for financial irregularities as Treasurer of the Navy."

Throughout his life, Wilberforce wrestled with his temper. He was capable of savaging those with whom he disagreed politically in the early years of his political career. Even family members in those years had felt the lash of his tongue. Wilberforce's temper mellowed following his great change, but he still struggled with it.

Wilberforce was sometimes prone to melancholy and admitted as much to close friends. He could become depressed and emotionally exhausted. On two occasions, he appears to have suffered a nervous breakdown. Understanding the pressures of his work, it is no wonder. However, in spite of the tremendous cost to him personally, he persevered when others might quit.

Throughout his years in political life, Wilberforce fought a running battle to stay on top of his correspondence. He was often buried in letters from various people and sometimes forgot where important letters were. He once disclosed to John Quincy Adams he was three weeks late in answering a letter because Adams's letter had gotten wedged into the top of a desk drawer and he had only just found it.

FAMILY MAN

His marriage to Barbara Spooner, in 1797, brought him much joy. Following Wilberforce's marriage in 1797, life in his household could be rather amusing. Meals served by woefully inefficient servants Wilberforce had hired out of pity were an adventure, because nobody ever knew what to expect. Not only that, but Wilberforce's home was also filled, like Sir Winston Churchill's, with pets of every description. It was a loving home and everyone who visited said so. On the other hand, the financial ineptitude of his oldest son in 1830 (reducing his parents to a peripatetic existence in their children's homes) and the death of his second daughter in 1832 caused his final years to be overshadowed by grief and poverty. (In time three of his four sons became Roman Catholics, one an adversary of Lord Shaftsbury, Wilberforce's successor in many ways).

BIRTH OF A CHRISTIAN POLITICIAN

Wilberforce was not a Christian when he came into Parliament for his home constituency of Hull and as the youngest member of the House of Commons. His aim was not to do good, but to achieve personal success. He confessed to a friend, "My own distinction was my darling object."

After his election as the MP for Yorkshire (one of the most coveted seats in the House of Commons), Wilberforce accompanied his sister Sally, his mother, and two of his cousins to the French Riviera (for the sake of Sally's health). He had also invited Isaac Milner, tutor at Queens' College, Cambridge, an acquaintance. Though friends counted "Wilber" both religious and moral, had he known that Milner's huge frame housed both a fine mathematical brain and a strong "methodistical" [evangelical] faith, it is unlikely he would have invited him. The combination was unimaginable in an English gentleman!

Milner's clear thought and winsome manner were effective advertisements for "serious" Christianity. Wilberforce had the quicker tongue, Milner the sharper mind. As they journeyed, they debated the evangelicalism of Wilberforce's youth. Slowly, Milner's arguments were taking their toll on Wilberforce's heart and mind. It started him on a spiritual quest.

On a trip to Europe, he met some Christians and read William Law's book *A Serious Call to a Devout and Holy Life*. The book touched him profoundly and made him doubt his unbelief.

He found himself moving closer towards Christianity, and this led him to ask himself "Can one serve God and one's nation in parliament?" He wondered whether the two goals might be mutually exclusive.

Over the next months, Wilberforce read Philip Doddridge's *The Rise and Progress of Religion in the Soul* (1745) beside an open Bible. His reading and conversations with Milner convinced him of wealth's emptiness, Christianity's truth and his own failure to embrace its radical demands. Outwardly, he looked ever confident, but inwardly he agonized. "I was filled with sorrow," he wrote. "I am sure that no human creature could suffer more than I did for some months."

All of this led to Wilberforce's conversion to Christianity. It was not a casual experience with him, but affected his whole being with evangelical fervor. This great spiritual change caused him to reevaluate his life and purpose. For a time he considered withdrawing from public life for the sake of his faith. He confided in his friend William Pitt, now Prime Minister. Pitt convinced him not to withdraw but to devote himself to the cause of Christ through politics.

Still, with "ten thousand doubts," he approached John Newton. The aging saint advised him, "It is hoped and believed that the Lord has raised you up for the good of his church and for the good of the nation."

He discussed the problem with John Newton, the hymn writer and former slave ship captain. They met in secret because the establishment frowned on evangelical Christians. In fact it would have been scandalous for an MP to be seen conversing with a Methodist at that time.

But secret or not, it was a meeting that changed Wilberforce, and in doing so, changed history. "When I came away, my mind was in a calm, tranquil state, more humbled, looking more devoutly up to God."

As a new convert to Christianity in 1784, William Wilberforce, a member of the House of Commons since 1780 at the age of 21, seriously considered getting out of politics to better pursue spiritual growth. But ex-slave trader John Newton, then a pastor, convinced him that his most important spiritual duty was to stay where he was in the rough and tumble of the political world and there live out his witness for Christ. On Sunday, October 28, 1787, Wilberforce had met with Rev. John Newton, who is best known today as the author of the hymn, Amazing Grace. The two friends talked for a long time. They spoke of the great needs that existed in Britain and the evils of the slave trade. Wilberforce now saw his path clearly. After Newton left, he took up his quill pen, and wrote in his diary: "God Almighty has set before me two great objects, the suppression of the slave trade and the reformation of manners [i.e. morals]."

Wilberforce's unnatural gloom finally lifted on Easter, 1786, "amidst the general chorus with which all nature seems on such a morning to be swelling the song of praise and thanksgiving." He believed his new life had begun. He had a purpose that energized him as never before.

His sense of vocation began growing within. "My walk is a public one," he wrote in his diary. "My business is in the world, and I must mix in the assemblies of men or quit the post which Providence seems to have assigned me." He also increasingly felt the burden of his calling: "A man who acts from the principles I profess," he later wrote, "reflects that he is to give an account of his political conduct at the judgment seat of Christ."

Newton, who was much older than Wilberforce, lived long enough to see the abolition of the slave trade in 1807. "At last," Wilberforce had written to Newton near the end, "[I] can join with you in the shout of victory." Twenty-six years later, Wilberforce experienced a similar joy of victory when he learned that slavery itself throughout the British Empire would be abolished.

Newton told Wilberforce: "God has raised you up for the good of the church and the good of the nation; maintain your friendship with Pitt, continue in Parliament, who knows that but for such a time as this God has brought you into public life and has a purpose for you." Newton helped Wilberforce to find his feet spiritually and set him on the path of service to humanity. Now Wilberforce knew what he should do with his life. It is the true duty of every man to promote the happiness of his fellow creatures to the utmost of his power.

FINDING HIS CAUSE

Wilberforce's conversion led to choose a good cause rather than promote his own career. Up until this time his interests were primarily self-centered, now his perspective was completely overhauled. He began casting about to see what he could do to make the most of his position and influence. After all, he believed God had so positioned him for a purpose, finding that purpose became the new passion of his life.

The greatest blight on British society was slavery. The ugly marks of slavery were everywhere and had seemingly touched everything. Wilberforce decided that the greatest evil facing the country was that people wanted to be able to own other people as their slaves. Wilberforce decided he would fight to end slavery.

The Abolitionist Movement at the time was weak and needed a champion in Parliament, someone who would bring an "Inquiry into the Slave Trade" before the House of Commons. It was unpopular throughout the country. Many believed Wilberforce was the man for the job, and although he felt unequal to the task and overwhelmed by the enormity of it, he took the request seriously.

In order to make a case against the slave trade Wilberforce first needed hard evidence and he began to work closely with a young abolitionist called Thomas Clarkson who had already done a lot of research into the treatment of slaves. Working together they could amass the needed evidence to make their case before the English populace.

The Society of Friends in Britain had been campaigning against the slave trade for many years. They had presented a petition to Parliament in 1783 and in 1787 had helped form the Society for the Abolition of the Slave Trade.

Wilberforce, along with Thomas Clarkson and Granville Sharp, was now seen as one of the leaders of the anti-slave

11

trade movement. Most of Wilberforce's Tory colleagues in the House of Commons were opposed to any restrictions on the slave trade, and at first he had to rely on the support of Whigs such as Charles Fox, Richard Brinsley Sheridan, William Grenville and Henry Brougham. When William Wilberforce presented his first bill to abolish the slave trade in 1791, it was easily defeated by 163 votes to 88.

Wilberforce refused to be beaten and in 1805, the House of Commons passed a bill that made it unlawful for any British subject to transport slaves, but the House of Lords blocked the measure.

In February, 1806, Lord Grenville formed a Whig administration. Grenville and his Foreign Secretary, Charles Fox, were strong opponents of the slave trade. Fox and Wilberforce led the campaign in the House of Commons, whereas Lord Grenville had the task of persuading the House of Lords to accept the measure.

Lord Grenville made a passionate speech where he argued that the trade was "contrary to the principles of justice, humanity and sound policy" and criticized fellow members for "not having abolished the trade long ago." When the vote was taken the Abolition of the Slave Trade bill was passed in the House of Lords by 41 votes to 20. In the House of Commons it was carried by 114 to 15 and it become law on March 25, 1807.

British captains who were caught continuing the trade were fined £100 for every slave found on board. However, this law did not stop the British slave trade. If slave ships were in danger of being captured by the British navy, captains often reduced the fines they had to pay by ordering the slaves to be thrown into the sea.

Some people involved in the anti-slave trade campaign, such as Thomas Fowell Buxton, argued that the only way to end the suffering of the slaves was to make slavery illegal. Wilberforce disagreed; he believed that at this time slaves were not ready to be granted their freedom. He pointed out in a pamphlet that he wrote in 1807 that: "It would be wrong to emancipate (the slaves). To grant freedom to them immediately would be to insure not only their masters' ruin, but also their own. They must (first) be trained and educated for freedom."

In 1823, Thomas Fowell Buxton formed the Society for the Mitigation and Gradual Abolition of Slavery. Buxton eventually persuaded Wilberforce to join his campaign but, as he had retired from the House of Commons in 1825, he did not play an important part in persuading Parliament to end slavery.

MAKING THE CASE AGAINST SLAVERY

His diary for the summer of 1786 charts his painful search for greater discipline and a clearer vocation. He flitted between humanitarian and local causes, between parliamentary and national reform. He studied to correct his Cambridge indolence. He practiced abstinence from alcohol and rigorous self-examination as befit, he believed, a "serious" Christian.

After one dinner with Pitt, he wrote in his diary about the "temptations of the table," meaning the endless stream of dinner parties filled with vain and useless conversation. "[They] disqualify me for every useful purpose in life, waste my time, impair my health, fill my mind with thoughts of resistance before and self-condemnation afterwards."

In early 1786, friends who were committed abolitionists had tentatively approached Wilberforce. They asked him to lead the parliamentary campaign for their cause. Even Pitt prodded him in this direction: "Wilberforce, why don't you give notice of a motion on the subject of the slave trade?" However, Wilberforce hesitated.

The slave trade in the late 1700s involved thousands of slaves, hundreds of ships, and millions of pounds; upon it depended the economies of Britain and much of Europe. Few were aware of the horrors of the so-called "Middle Passage" across the Atlantic, where an estimated one out of four slaves died.

Some Englishmen, including John Wesley and Thomas Clarkson, had taken steps to mitigate the evil. Yet few in England shared the abolitionists' sense that slavery was a great social evil. Some presumed that slaves were a justifiable necessity or that they deserved their plight.

For Wilberforce light began to dawn slowly during his 27th year. His diary for Sunday, October 28, 1787, shows with extraordinary clarity the fruit of prolonged study, prayer and conversation. He realized the need for "some reformer of the nation's morals, who should raise his voice in the high places of the land and do within the church and nearer the throne what Wesley has accomplished in the meeting and among the multitude."

Later he reflected on his decision about slavery: "So enormous, so dreadful, so irremediable did the trade's wickedness appear that my own mind was completely made up for abolition. Let the consequences be what they would; I from this time determined that I would never rest until I had effected its abolition."

After much consideration and prayer on the matter, Wilberforce decided to attack the slavers' own case in favor of their trade. It might seem incredible today, but the slavers argued that theirs was a moral trade because they were trying to help people captured in African wars, who were otherwise going to be executed and they were taking them to a safe place and a new life. Only a politician could call an evil good.

Wilberforce and his friends began thoroughly to research these outlandish claims.

They sent people to Africa to see what conditions were like and they put others on slave ships to document what took place. They sent them to the West Indies and even to the southern United States. The researchers came back with reams of information providing the facts Wilberforce used in his first passionate speech in Parliament.

It was a speech that changed history, because after reciting the facts for three hours Wilberforce challenged the lawmakers: "Having heard all of this you may choose to look the other way but you can never again say that you did not know."

Until then it was possible for people in Britain to say that they did not know the truth about slavery. And they were right. Today with 24/7 news coverage, we forget that Britain did not have the information needed to thoughtfully discuss the slavery question. Those involved in the slave trade saw to it that much of the information about the trade was not made public. Wilberforce's challenge was to make public as much as possible what was really happening in the slave trade. His tactic proved successful, although it took time and much hard work to overcome many obstacles.

When the slave ships left Britain, their cargo was manufactured goods not slaves. They picked up the slaves in Africa and took them to America—and for the people in Britain, out of sight was out of mind.

Some of the slave ship captains, appalled by what was going on, brought extra information to Wilberforce, so he could expose what was happening on the ships and reveal that many slaves were dying on the journey. Some ships had even been sunk with slaves still manacled and chained, rather than to get caught and have to pay a fine.

Wilberforce faced many daunting obstacles while in politics. During the French Revolution and the war with France that soon followed, many in England—particularly supporters of the slave trade—accused Wilberforce of being in league with the revolutionaries. He endured formidable opposition from the royal family. George III once cut him at a royal levee—walking past him in a receiving line without a word or glance—and several of the royal dukes spoke against him in Parliament. No less a person than Lord Nelson attacked him, saying: "I was bred in the good old school and taught to appreciate the value of our West Indian possessions, and neither in the field nor the senate shall their just rights be infringed, while I have an arm to fight in their defense or a tongue to launch my voice against the damnable doctrine of Wilberforce and his hypocritical allies."

Wilberforce's resolve in the face of the challenges he confronted can be best thought of as courage under fire and debility. Sometimes, the taking of a stand on principle severely strained his friendship with Prime Minister Pitt, at other times, his health would suffer greatly. In spite of everything, he carried forward the work of abolition and the other good works he championed.

Far from being a Machiavellian political intriguer who carried all before him and left opponents floating in his wake, Wilberforce chose instead the harder path of trying to persuade those with whom he disagreed to join him. At times, he was laughed at, spat upon, physically assaulted or vilified in the press, but to his credit he persevered. Service to something larger than self, and a binding commitment to the Golden Rule, sustained and drove him.

Wilberforce was initially optimistic, naively so, and expressed "no doubt of our success." He sought to stem the flow of slaves from Africa by international accord. The strength of his feelings and the support of prominent politicians like Pitt, Edmund Burke and Charles Fox blinded him to the enormity of his task.

WILBERFORCE AND WESLEY

John Newton was not Wilberforce's only source of spiritual comfort. He had a group of people around him who were encouragers, most notably John Wesley—the founder of Methodism and the greatest preacher of his day. The Wesley brothers deeply influenced Wilberforce's political activities as well as his spiritual development.

From his deathbed, John Wesley wrote these words to him, "I see not how you can go through your glorious enterprise in opposing that execrable villainy, which is the scandal of religion, of England, and of human nature. Unless God has raised you up for this very thing, you will be worn out by the opposition of men and devils. But if God be for you, who can be against you?"

In fact, the very last letter that John Wesley wrote was to William Wilberforce, telling him to carry on with his appointed task.

Dear Sir:

Unless the divine power has raised you up to be as Athanasius contra mundum, I see not how you can go through your glorious enterprise in opposing that execrable villainy which is the scandal of religion, of England, and of human nature. Unless God has raised you up for this very thing, you will be worn out by the opposition of men and devils. But if God be for you, who can be against you? Are all of them together stronger than God? O be not weary of well doing! Go on, in the name of God and in the power of his might, till even American slavery (the vilest that ever saw the sun) shall vanish away before it.

Reading this morning a tract wrote by a poor African, I was particularly struck by that circumstance that a man who has a black skin, being wronged or outraged by a white man, can have no redress; it being a "law" in our colonies that the oath of a black against a white goes for nothing. What villainy is this?

That he who has guided you from youth up may continue to strengthen you in this and all things, is the prayer of, dear sir,

Your affectionate servant,
John Wesley

In May, 1788, Wilberforce had recovered from another of his periodic bouts of illness to introduce a 12-point motion to Parliament indicting the trade. He and Thomas Clarkson (whom Wilberforce praised as central to the cause's success) had thoroughly researched and now publicized the trade's physical atrocities. But Parliament wanted to maintain the status quo, and the motion was defeated.

The campaign and opposition intensified. Planters, businessmen, ship owners, traditionalists and even the Crown opposed the movement. Many feared personal financial ruin and nationwide recession if the trade ceased. Wilberforce was vilified. Admiral Horatio Nelson castigated "the damnable doctrine of Wilberforce and his hypocritical allies." One of Wilberforce's friends wrote, fearing he would one day read of Wilberforce being "carbonated [broiled] by West Indian planters, barbecued by African merchants, and eaten by Guinea captains."

Wilberforce's spirit was indomitable, his enthusiasm palpable. As the slave owners' agent in Jamaica wrote, "It is necessary to watch him, as he is blessed with a very sufficient quantity of that enthusiastic spirit, which is so far from yielding that it grows more vigorous from blows."

The pathway to abolition was fraught with difficulty. Vested interest, parliamentary filibustering, entrenched bigotry, international politics, slave unrest, personal sickness and political fear—all combined to frustrate the movement. It would take years before Wilberforce would see success.

A DANIEL IN THE LION'S DEN

Wilberforce was brilliant at public relations, and devised radical new ways of bringing his cause to public attention. One of his master strokes was created with the potter Josiah Wedgewood. They struck a brooch that depicted a slave and a slave owner and at the bottom of the brooch was the inscription: "Am I not a man and a brother?" The brooch really touched people's hearts, and became a style icon that women would wear to fashionable evenings in town.

Another of his public relations coups was to get the famous poet William Cowper to write two poems about the slave trade, the Negro's Complaint and Pity for Poor Africans. These are included in this collection.

It was the ex-slave trader turned evangelical minister, John Newton who helped Wilberforce see that although he had suffered a crushing defeat, God was indeed using him, progress had been made and Wilberforce needed to stick with the campaign.

Newton quoted the Bible story of Daniel in the lions' den. Daniel, Newton explained, was a public man like Wilberforce, and, like Wilberforce, found himself in great difficulty. But Daniel trusted in the Lord and was faithful and therefore, though he had enemies, none could prevail against him. "The God whom you serve continually is able to preserve and deliver you, he will see you through." This proved to be just the advice Wilberforce needed.

Strengthened by this encouragement and his supporters, Wilberforce continued the fight, recovering from defeat after defeat over the following eleven years.

But his time was coming; outside Parliament, a tremendous popular campaign was raising the profile of the abolitionist cause.

On February 23, 1807, Wilberforce's latest anti-slavery motion was debated in Parliament. When Wilberforce realized that the majority of the speeches were in favor and that he was going to win, he bowed his head and wept. At four o'clock in the morning the Commons voted by 283 to 16 to abolish the slave trade. It had taken twenty years to get this far. But there was still another battle to win. The capturing, transporting and selling of slaves was now illegal in Britain and its colonies, but existing slaves remained in captivity.

Wilberforce kept up this fight for their emancipation — but it was by no means his only project. Wilberforce was involved in educational reform, prison reform, health care reform to improve life for the poor and their children.

In 1823, he wrote his famous Appeal on Behalf of the Negro Slaves, which led to the influential Anti-Slavery Society being formed.

EMANCIPATION OF SLAVES

Wilberforce continued with his work after 1807, and his concern about slavery led him to found the African Institution, the aim of which was to improve the conditions of slaves in the West Indies. He was also instrumental in developing the Sierra Leone project to help with the eventual goal of taking Christianity to West Africa. Wilberforce's position as the leading evangelical in Parliament was acknowledged, and he was by now the foremost member of the so-called Clapham Sect, along with his brother-in-law Henry Thornton and Edward Eliot. Because most of the group held evangelical Christian convictions, they were dubbed "the Saints."

By 1820, after a period of ill health and a decision to limit his public activities, Wilberforce was still laboring for the eventual emancipation of all slaves, and in 1821 asked Thomas Powell Buxton to take over the leadership of the campaign in the Commons.

Wilberforce published his *Appeal to the Religion, Justice and Humanity of the Inhabitants of the British Empire in Behalf of the Negro Slaves in the West Indies* in early 1823, in which he claimed that the moral and spiritual condition of the slaves stemmed directly from their slavery, and claimed that total emancipation was morally and ethically justified, and a matter of national duty before God.

1823 also saw the formation of the Society for the Mitigation and Gradual Abolition of Slavery (later the Anti-Slavery Society) and on May 15, 1823, Buxton moved a resolution in Parliament against slavery, a debate in which Wilberforce took an active part. There followed subsequent debates on March 16, and June 11, 1823, at which Wilberforce made his last speech in the House of Commons.

In 1824, Wilberforce suffered a serious illness, and early the following year resigned his parliamentary seat. He moved to a small estate in Mill Hill, north of London in 1826. This resulted in his health improving somewhat, although in his retirement he continued his passionate belief in the anti-slavery cause, to which he had given his life, and maintained an active correspondence with his extensive circle of friends, many of whom he continued to visit.

By 1833, his health had begun to decline, and he suffered a severe attack of influenza from which he never fully recovered. On July 26, 1833, he heard, with much rejoicing, that the bill for the abolition of slavery had finally passed its third reading in the Commons. On the following day, he grew much weaker, and died early on the morning of July 29. One month later, Parliament passed the Slavery Abolition Act that gave all slaves in the British Empire their freedom.

William Wilberforce was buried in Westminster Abbey on August 3, 1833. The funeral was attended by many members from both Houses of Parliament, as well as many members of the public, and the pallbearers including the Lord Chancellor and the Duke of Gloucester.

A statue to the memory of one of Britain's greatest parliamentarians was erected in Westminster Abbey in 1840, and a memorial column was erected in Hull in 1834.

OTHER WORKS

The abolition of slavery was not Wilberforce's only concern. The second "great object" of Wilberforce's life was the reformation of the nation's morals. Early in 1787, he conceived of a society that would work, as a royal proclamation put it, "for the encouragement of piety and virtue; and for the preventing of vice, profaneness, and immorality." It eventually became known as the Society for the Suppression of Vice. Enlisting support from leading figures in church and state—and King George III— Wilberforce made private morality a matter of public concern.

Laws restricting drinking, swearing and gaming on Sundays were enforced. "All loose and licentious prints, books and publications" were suppressed, including Thomas Paine's *The Age of Reason*. Wilberforce was criticized for his "priggish" concerns, yet John Pollock, a recent biographer, wrote, "The reformation of manners grew into Victorian virtues and Wilberforce touched the world when he made goodness fashionable."

It has been estimated that Wilberforce—dubbed "the prime minister of a cabinet of philanthropists"—was at one time active in support of 69 philanthropic causes. He gave away a fourth of his annual income to the poor. He also gave an annuity to Charles Wesley's widow from 1792 until her death in 1822. He fought the cause of "climbing boys" (chimney sweeps) and single mothers. He sought the welfare of soldiers, sailors, and animals, and established Sunday schools and orphanages for "criminal poor children." His homes were havens for the marginalized and dispossessed.

Targeting the powerful as the agents of change, Wilberforce made common cause with Hannah More, the evangelical playwright, whose *Thoughts on the Manners of the Great* appeared in 1787. "To expect to reform the poor while the opulent are corrupt," she wrote, "is to throw odors [perfume] on the stream while the springs are poisoned."

Clapham, a leafy village south of London, became a base for a number of these influential people, who became known as the "Clapham Sect." These bankers and diplomats, legislators, and businessmen shared a commitment to a godly life in public service. Their "vital" and "practical" Christianity expressed Wilberforce's vision of an integrated evangelicalism committed to a spiritual and a social gospel. The group's reputation for philanthropy and evangelical fervor spread. One politician warned, "I would counsel my Lords and Bishops to keep their eyes upon that holy village."

Wilberforce's public struggles and success must be set against the background of his private joys and pains.

His book, *A Practical View of the Prevailing Religious System of Professed Christians in the Higher and Middle Classes of this Country Contrasted with Real Christianity* was published in 1797 and sold well for many years.

Most of England had become unchurched by the 18th century, and Wilberforce was determined to draw people back into the Christian faith. However, he did not just want people to return to a Christianity limited to church on Sundays; he wanted them to embrace a Christianity that would change the whole fabric of British society.

What he really wanted to do was to reform manners— not social customs, but the way in which people thought of virtue. Nowadays we might call that a project for making goodness fashionable. Wilberforce claimed, "God Almighty has set before me two great objects, the suppression of the slave trade and the reformation of manners."

He worked with friends inside and outside of Parliament, bishops, friends in high places, and influential people throughout British society. He worked with the poor, he worked to establish educational reform, prison reform, health care reform and to limit the number of hours children were required to work in factories. Wilberforce believed that he and his supporters should attempt to cure every social ill in the country.

To deal with many of these problems they established organizations that would work to improve or rectify the particular social injustice that they were dealing with.

Wilberforce not only brought his faith into his public life but into his private life, too. He used his large income for good causes, donating generously to charity and cutting the rents he charged the tenants on his land.

WRITINGS

In April, 1797, Wilberforce completed *Practical View of the Prevailing Religious System of Professed Christians in the Higher and Middle Classes of this Country Contrasted With Real Christianity*, which he had been working on since

1793, and was an exposition of New Testament doctrine and teachings and a call for revival of the Christian religion, in view of what he saw as the moral decline of the nation. It was an influential work and illustrates, far more than any other of his writings, his own personal testimony and the views, which inspired him in his life's work.

After the death of Fox in September, 1806, Wilberforce was again re-elected for Yorkshire and spent the latter part of the year writing *A Letter on the Abolition of the Slave Trade*, an apologetic essay in which he summarized the huge volume of evidence against the trade that he and Clarkson had accumulated over two decades. Published on January 31, 1807, it formed the basis for the final phase of the abolition campaign.

In early 1823 Wilberforce published his *Appeal to the Religion, Justice and Humanity of the Inhabitants of the British Empire in Behalf of the Negro Slaves in the West Indies*, in which he claimed that the moral and spiritual condition of the slaves stemmed directly from their slavery, and claimed that total emancipation was morally and ethically justified, and a matter of national duty before God.

Wilberforce's life was not without criticism. Some see in his sons' five-volume *Life* muted praise of both his evangelicalism and his parenting. Opponents of abolition bitterly denounced both his character and his cause. A Wimbledon man, Anthony Fearon, attempted blackmail (causing Wilberforce to write, "At all events, he must not be permitted to publish"), but the precise grounds are not known.

Through all this, Wilberforce drew spiritual and intellectual strength from the Bible and the Puritans (such as Richard Baxter, John Owen, and Jonathan Edwards), and built his evangelical faith on a mildly Calvinist foundation.

Philip Doddridge's *Rise and Progress of Religion in the Soul* continued to shape his spirituality: daily self-examination, and extended times of prayer, regular Communions and fasting, morning and evening devotions, and times of solitude. He also paid careful attention to God's providential provision in his life, the needs of others, and his own mortality.

For all of Wilberforce's appeal to "real" and "vital" Christianity, especially in his best selling *A Practical View of the Prevailing Religious System ... Contrasted with Real Christianity* (1797), he did not embrace a dull, joyless legalism. His personality alone was too lively for that. As he once wrote to a relative, "My grand objection to the religious system still held by many who declare themselves orthodox churchmen ... is that it tends to render Christianity so much a system of prohibitions rather than of privilege and hopes ... and religion is made to wear a forbidding and gloomy air."

Three days before he died, a gravely ill Wilberforce (1759-1833) received word that Parliament had voted to abolish slavery itself throughout Britain's colonies. When he passed away, he did so safe in the knowledge that he had done all he could do for the sons and daughters of Africa. He had labored for 46 years.

Politicians from both houses of Parliament and from all parties petitioned that Wilberforce be buried in Westminster Abbey, a rare honor for a commoner. The petition was granted. Memorials were planned. Testimonials were given. The nation genuinely felt his loss. "No one," it was said, "had ever done more to elevate and ennoble English life." In America, the distinguished philanthropist Caspar Morris wrote, "Not one nation, but the whole human family participated in the benefit [Wilberforce] conferred on his fellow men."

Gallery

WILLIAM WILBERFORCE
1759–1833

Various portraits of William Wilberforce throughout his life.

In the 1780s, slavery in the plantations of the West Indies was the unseen evil. Eleven million human beings had been captured and taken from Africa to the West Indies to work in slavery and bondage. Britain had the biggest portion of the slave trade.

Many of the human beings were thrown overboard alive so that ship owners could collect insurance.

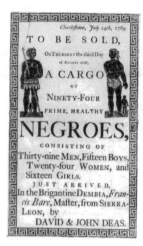

Typical handbill for a
slave auction.

Slave ship unloading its precious
cargo.

A sketch depicting the celebration of the abolition of slavery by
the colored people in the District of Columbia, April 19, 1866.

Hannah More was a
member of the
Clapham Group.

When Wilberforce died in 1833, Parliament resolved that he
should be buried in Westminster Abbey. His grave is next to Pitt
in the north transept and in 1840 a statue, by Samuel Joseph,
was set up in the north choir aisle.

Left & above: This
statue of
Wilberforce was
moved to High
Street from its
original location on
Dock Bridge.

A close friend of Wilberforce's, John Newton was a reformed slave-trader, who is best known as the composer of the popular hymn Amazing Grace.

William Pitt and Wilberforce were contemporaries at Cambridge. They became friendly during the parliamentary election of 1780, and soon after, they became close and intimate friends.

The Wilberforce seat on the grounds of Holwood, erected in 1802 and inscribed with an extract from Wilberforce's diary of 1787 reporting his meeting with William Pitt and their decision to abolish slavery in the British Empire.

Chapter Two

THE CLAPHAM GROUP:
THEY SET OUT TO
CHANGE THEIR WORLD

If you had money and influence, how would you use them? A group of well-heeled and well-placed Englishmen and women had the chance to answer that question at the end of the eighteenth century. Their decision is instructive. It changed their world.

A porcelain cameo by Josiah Wedgwood the potter (whose name is still known for fine china!). A Slave asks, "Am I not a man and a brother?" Used by Claphamites as a visual aid in their efforts against slavery.

Lampooned in their own day as "the saints," this group of prominent and wealthy individuals was known as "the Clapham Sect." They were named for Clapham, a village south of London, where most moved in evangelical Anglican circles. Busy professionals, all of them, they still made time for Christian action and gave liberally and effectively to worthy causes. Their foremost endeavor was to rid the world of slavery.

POLITICIAN CONVERTED

William Wilberforce was the most visible of them. Once a social gadfly, a highly visible member of Parliament, always a close friend to Prime Minister William Pitt, he became a passionate Christian. At 26 years of age, he and his friend the Reverend Isaac Milner toured Europe. To while away the tedium of the trip, they read Philip Doddridge's *Rise and Progress of Religion in the Soul*. Wilberforce realized that in the truest sense of the word he was not a Christian. He had never died to himself. Now he submitted his life to Christ. Immediately he became concerned to evangelize those around him. He wondered if he should not resign his seat in Parliament. John Newton, author of the hymn Amazing Grace, convinced him to stay and use his position for good. He suggested that Wilberforce might even attempt to abolish slavery. More and more the issue of slavery presented itself to the gifted Parliamentarian. Other leaders who shared his high sense of responsibility to God gathered around him, meeting in the Clapham home of the banker Henry Thornton.

Joining them was the lawyer Granville Sharp (who had already won a decision affirming that slavery was illegal in England); John Shore (Lord Teignmouth), sometime Governor-General of India; Charles Grant, a powerful member of the East India Council; Zachary Macaulay, an estate manager and businessman; James Stephen, who sat in court; and literary celebrity and educator Hannah More.

They combined their efforts to create public opinion and exert pressure on the government. They educated the public by issuing a journal, writing letters, spearheading petition drives, distributing pamphlets, speaking, and making every effort to persuade those with whom they had personal influence.

With Pitt's support, Wilberforce introduced a bill to abolish the slave trade. The bill failed despite his eloquence and careful research. Wilberforce determined to present the measure again the following year. It was again unsuccessful. Year after year the Clapham group labored on, often at a high cost to themselves. Macaulay, for example, devoted himself so completely to the task that he gave up night after night of sleep, neglected his business and lost much of his substantial fortune. Henry Thornton sometimes contributed over 80 percent of his income to charity. Tender-minded Ramsay, who had reluctantly made public the slaver atrocities he had witnessed, was hounded to death by malicious accusations. Wilberforce himself suffered a nervous breakdown and was so sick that he faced death. His life was threatened by the opposition. Once, another member of Parliament felt compelled to protect him, loaded pistol in hand. Real Christianity, they discovered, comes with a price tag.

NOT SINGLE-ISSUE ADVOCATES

The Clapham Sect turned their attention to multiple projects, which promised to transform morals and society. They worked to ban bull fighting and bear baiting, to suspend the lottery, and to improve prisons. Their support for factory acts bettered working conditions. At their instigation, Sierra Leone was founded to provide a home for refugee slaves. Zachary Macaulay became first governor and drove himself beyond exhaustion for the good of the colony.

It was the Claphamites which funded Hannah More's schools. Additionally, they had a big part in the formation of church, Bible, tract and mission societies. Against the opposition of the East India Company, this valiant band fought to allow missionaries in India. Parliament eventually agreed. It was thanks to the Clapham group that chaplains were provided to East India company employees.

Meanwhile, they plugged away at their primary cause: the abolition of slavery. In 1807, eighteen years after the first vote, these Christians rejoiced as Parliament abolished the slave trade. The members of the Clapham Sect supposed that slavery would wither away of its own accord. It did not. Wilberforce then introduced a bill to obtain the emancipation of all British slaves. It was defeated. He introduced it again. And again.

The years rolled past. Emancipation finally passed in England just a few days before Wilberforce died in 1833 at the age of 74.

It is arguable that this handful of Christians, publicly living their faith, helped avert tragedy in Britain. Their concern for the underdog may have helped forestall a revolution, such as the one that swept through France.

Their story stands out in the annals of Christian history as a striking example of how God can use a company of believers who work together, sacrifice their time and resources, and patiently persist in faith against seemingly insurmountable odds.

FASCINATING FACTS

• Wilberforce wasn't much to look at. Boswell described him as a "shrimp" who, as he was speaking, "grew into a whale."

• Zachary Macaulay's zeal for abolition led him to take passage on an African slaver so that he might witness firsthand the horrors of the trade. So extensive was his knowledge of the slave trade, the others would seek answers by "looking it up in the Macaulay."

• When Wilberforce wrote A Practical View of the Prevailing Religious System ... Contrasted to Real Christianity, the publisher issued only 500 copies, supposing it would never sell. But by 1826 it had gone through 15 editions in England and 25 in America.

• For helping a slave escape while in an English harbor, Granville Sharp was charged with unlawfully detaining the property of another. England's top legal authorities said that slaves were property. Sharp carefully researched and argued the issue. The judges ruled that "as soon as a slave sets his foot upon English territory he becomes free."

IN HIS OWN WORDS

Two Selections from Wilberforce's *Practical View of the Prevailing Religious System of Professed Christians in the Higher and Middle Classes of this Country Contrasted With Real Christianity*

I apprehend the essential practical characteristic of true Christians to be this: that relying on the promises to repenting sinners of acceptance through the Redeemer, they have renounced and abjured all other masters, and have cordially and unreservedly devoted themselves to God ... It is now their determined purpose to yield themselves without reserve to the reasonable service of the Rightful Sovereign. They are not their own: their bodily and mental faculties, their natural and acquired endowments, their substance, their authority, their time, their influence, all these they consider as belonging to them ... to be consecrated to the honor of God and employed in his service.

ON MIGHT OR RIGHT?

I must confess ... that my own solid hopes for the well-being of my country depend, not so much on her navies and armies, nor on the wisdom of her rulers, nor on the spirit of her people, as on the persuasion that she still contains many who love and obey the gospel of Christ.

THE CLAPHAM GROUP

They challenged the whole moral climate of their times and changed their world! Their efforts ranged across a wide spectrum of issues, including slavery, missions, prison reform, public immorality, and the needs of the poor.

MEMBERS

Name of Member	Date	Position in Life	Reason for Joining
Gisbourne, Thomas	1758-1846	Clergyman and Author	Friendship with Wilberforce and others
Grant, Charles	1746-1823	Business administrator	Ties with other members
Macaulay, Zachary	1768-1838	Estate manager, colonial governor	Evangelical zeal
More, Hannah	1745-1835	Playwright, and educator	Evangelical zeal
Sharp, Granville	1735-1813	Scholar and administrator	Continuation of his earlier abolitionism
Smith, Sir William	1756-1835	Parliamentarian	Tender heartedness
Stephen, James	1758-1832	Master of Chancery	Shocked by cruelty to Barbados slaves
Teignmouth, Lord	1751-1834	Governor-General of India	Evangelical zeal
Thornton, Henry	1760-1815	Banker	Marriage into Wilberforce's family

Venn, John	1759-1813	Rector of Clapham	Zeal and association with Wilberforce, etc.
Wilberforce, William	1759-1833	Parliamentarian	Evangelical zeal

A DOZEN CHARACTERISTICS
(Editor's Notebook)

We produced a little video program a few years ago, along with a discussion guide on the life of William Wilberforce and the Clapham group. In preparing the film it struck me how the Claphamites demonstrated the difference that a handful of Christian people can make. They are a kind of case study for effecting social change. Briefly, here are a dozen characteristics they exemplified:.

1. Set clear and specific goals
2. Researched carefully to produce reliable and irrefutable evidence
3. Built a committed support community. The battle could not be carried on alone.
4. Refused to accept setbacks as final defeats
5. Committed to the struggle for the long haul, even if it took decades.
6. Focused on issues, not allowing opponents' vicious attacks on their person to distract them, or provoke them into similar response.
7. Empathized with opponents' position so that meaningful interaction could take place.
8. Accepted incremental gains when everything could not be achieved at once.
9. Cultivated grassroots support when rebuffed by those in power.

10. Transcended a single-issue mentality by addressing issues as part of overall moral climate.

11. Worked through recognized channels without resort to dirty tactics or violence.

12. Proceeded with a sense of mission and conviction that God would providentially guide if they were truly acting in His service.

Part 2

EXCERPTS FROM

A Practical View of the Prevailing Religious System of Professed Christians in the Higher and Middle Classes, Contrasted with Real Christianity

BY WILLIAM WILBERFORCE

Chapter Three

INTRODUCTION AND
INADEQUATE CONCEPTIONS OF THE
IMPORTANCE OF CHRISTIANITY

INTRODUCTION

The main object I have in view with regard to this book is not to convince the skeptic or to answer the arguments of persons who avowedly oppose the fundamental doctrines of Christianity, but to point out the scanty and erroneous system followed by the bulk of those who belong to the class of orthodox Christians and to contrast their defective schemes with a representation of what I understand to be real Christianity.

It has often filled me with deep concern to observe in these people scarcely any distinct knowledge of the real nature and principles of the religion which many profess. The subject is of infinite importance; therefore, let it not be driven out of our minds by the bustle or dissipations of life.

This present scene, with all its cares and all its frivolities, will soon be rolled away, and "we must all stand before the judgment seat of Christ" (Romans 14:10). This awful consideration prompts me to express myself with greater freedom than I might otherwise use. This consideration will also justify my frankness, and will ensure a serious and patient perusal of what I write.

If what I state here should appear needlessly austere and rigid, I want to say that I do not want to be condemned without a fair inquiry as to whether or not my statements in this book accord with the language of the sacred writings (the Holy Bible). To that test I refer with confidence; and it must be conceded by those who admit the authority of Scripture, that from the decision of the Word of God there can be no appeal.

POPULAR NOTIONS OF THE IMPORTANCE OF CHRISTIANITY

Before we consider particular defects in the religious system that is followed by the bulk of professed Christians, it may be proper to point out the very inadequate conception they entertain with regard to the importance of Christianity in general and its superior excellence.

If we listen to the conversations of nominal Christians, we find that virtue is praised and vice is censured. Likewise, we find that piety is applauded, and profaneness is condemned. So far all is well. But let anyone, who would not be deceived by "barren generalities," examine the situation more closely, and he or she will find that not to Christianity in particular, but, at best, to religion in general, perhaps to mere morality, their homage is being paid.

Christianity, as distinct from these other approaches, seems to elude them. Their views of it have been so cursory and superficial, that, far from discerning its characteristic essence, they have little more than perceived those exterior circumstances that distinguish it from other forms of religion. There are some few facts, and perhaps some leading doctrines and principles of which they cannot be wholly ignorant, but they are seemingly unaware of the consequences, relations, and practical uses of these.

As we take a look at their plan of life and their ordinary conduct and, not to speak at present of general inattention to things of a religious nature, let us ask, ourselves how we can discern the points of discrimination between them and professed unbelievers?

We live in an age in which infidelity abounds. Do we observe in the nominal Christian any remarkable care to instruct their children in the principles of the faith which they profess and to furnish their children with arguments for the defense of it? They would blush, as their child comes out into the world, to think of him or her as being defective in any branch of the knowledge or accomplishments that belong to his or her particular station in life or field of study and endeavor; accordingly, these are cultivated with diligence.

But the study of Christianity has formed no part of the education of most children, and their attachment to it, where any attachment to it exists at all, is merely the result of having been born in a Christian country. When such is the hereditary religion handed down from generation to generation, it cannot surprise us to observe young men and women who are shaken by frivolous objections and irreverent quibbling.

Let us beware of all this before it is too late. No one can say what may be the painful results, at a time when the free and unrestrained communications subsisting among the several ranks and classes of society, so much favors the general diffusion of the sentiments of the higher orders of Christianity.

It cannot be expected, that they who are so little attentive to this great object in the education of their children, should be more attentive in other parts of their conduct, where they are less strongly stimulated by affection and less obviously loaded with responsibility. They are, therefore, little regardful of the state of Christianity in their own country and very indifferent about communicating the light of divine truth to the nations that "sit in darkness."

But religion, it may be replied, is not noisy and ostentatious; it is modest and private in its nature; it resides in a man's own bosom, and shuns the observation of the multitude.

From this transient and distant view, then, let us approach a little closer to their discourse and listen to the unreserved conversation that takes place during their confidential hours. Here, if anywhere, we may ascertain the true principles of their regards and aversions and discover the scale by which they measure the good and evil of life. Here, however, you will discover few or no traces of Christianity. The religion founded by Jesus scarcely finds a place amidst the many objects of their hopes and fears and joys and sorrows.

They may be grateful, perhaps, for health, talents, affluence, and other blessings, but they scarcely see these things as the bounty of Providence; or, if they mention it at all, it is referred to coldly and formally.

Let their conversation take a graver turn. At length, their religion, modest and retired as it is, must be expected to disclose itself; however, you will look in vain for the religion of Jesus. Their standard of right and wrong is not the standard of the Gospel. They approve and condemn according to a different rule; they advance principles and maintain opinions altogether opposite to the genius and character of Christianity.

THE WORD OF GOD—THE HOLY SCRIPTURES

The truth is that their opinions on these subjects are not formed from the perusal of the Word of God. Their Bibles are unopened, and they would be wholly ignorant of its contents, except for what they hear occasionally at church. Or they may recall some faint traces from the lessons of their earliest childhood. How different and how contradictory would be the two systems of mere morals, of which the one should be formed from the commonly received maxims of the Christian world, and the other from the study of the holy Scriptures!

It is a waste of time to multiply arguments in order to prove how criminal the voluntary ignorance of which we have been speaking must appear in the sight of God. It must be confessed by all who believe that we are accountable to God for everything. This is my concern, that we shall have to answer hereafter to the Almighty for all the means and opportunities we have had to improve ourselves and to promote the happiness of others.

When we are summoned to give an account of our stewardship, we shall be called upon to answer for the use we have made of our bodily organs and how we have applied the means of relieving the wants and necessities of our fellow-creatures. Likewise, we shall have to give an account regarding how we have exercised the nobler and more exalted faculties of our nature—of invention, judgment, and memory; and for our employment of all the instruments and opportunities of diligent application, serious reflection, and honest decision we have been provided!

To what subject might we in all reason be expected to apply more earnestly than that which involves our eternal interests? When God has of His goodness vouchsafed to grant us such abundant means of instruction concerning that which we are most concerned to know, how great must be the guilt and how awful the punishment that results from voluntary ignorance! We have the Bible as our standard in all the matters of our lives.

And why, it may be asked, are we in this pursuit alone to expect knowledge without inquiry and success without endeavor? The whole analogy of nature inculcates within us a different lesson; and our own judgments, in matters of temporal interest and worldly policy, confirm the truth of those suggestions.

As bountiful as the hand of Providence is, its gifts are not so bestowed as to seduce us into indolence; rather, they are given to rouse us to exertion, and no one expects to attain to the height of learning, arts, power, or wealth without vigorous resolution, strenuous diligence, and steady perseverance. However, it seems that many expect to be Christians without labor, study, or inquiry. This is all the more preposterous, because Christianity, being a revelation from God and not the invention of man, provides us with new relations and their correspondent duties. It also presents doctrines, motives, practical principles, and rules for our lives. These are so new in their nature and supreme in their excellence that we cannot reasonably expect to become proficient in the practice of Christianity by the accidental intercourses of life, as one might learn, insensibly, the maxims of worldly policy or a mere human scheme of morals.

The diligent perusal of the holy Scriptures helps us to see the extent of our ignorance. We should cease to be deceived by superficial appearances and to confound the Gospel of Christ with the systems of philosophers. We should become impressed with the weighty truth of the Scriptures, so much forgotten and never to be too strongly insisted on, that Christianity calls on us, as we value our immortal souls, not merely to be religious and moral, but to believe and live by the doctrines, the principles, and the practice of the precepts of Christ.

Christianity is always represented in Scripture as the grand, unparalleled instance of God's bounty to mankind. It was graciously held forth in the original promise to our first parents; it was predicted by a long, continued series of prophets; it has always been the subject of their prayers, inquiries, and longing expectations. In a world which opposed and persecuted these patriarchs and prophets of the faith, their source of peace, hope, and consolation was found in the truths of God's Word. Jesus, the desire of all nations came to show us how to live. A multitude of the heavenly host hailed His coming and proclaimed His character: "Glory to God in the highest, on earth peace, good will towards men" (Luke 2:14).

The essential nature of Christianity is everywhere represented in Scripture by such figures and examples as may most deeply impress on us a sense of its value. It is spoken of as light from darkness, release from prison, deliverance from captivity, and life from death. "Lord, now lettest thou thy servant depart in peace, for mine eyes have seen thy salvation" (Luke 2:30). This was the exclamation with which it was welcomed by the pious Simeon; and it was universally received and professed, among the early converts, with thankfulness and joy. At one time, the communication of it is promised as a reward; at another, the loss of it is threatened as a punishment.

In spite of the brevity of the prayer that was taught to us by our blessed Savior (the Lord's Prayer), the general extension of the Kingdom of Christ constitutes one of its leading petitions.

We should be filled with exalted conceptions of the importance of Christianity by such descriptions and verbal images as these! That's why we should study the Scriptures carefully, "line upon line, and precept upon precept" (Isaiah 28:10). Thus predicted, thus prayed and longed for, thus announced and characterized and rejoiced in, we scarcely accept this heavenly treasure that has been poured into our laps in such rich abundance! All too often, we turn from it coldly, or, at best, we possess it negligently, as a thing of no account or estimation. But a due sense of its inherent value would be assuredly impressed on us by the diligent study of the Word of God, that blessed repository of divine truth and consolation. Thence it is that we are to learn our obligations and our duty — what we are to believe and what we are to practice. We must peruse and study this sacred volume on a daily basis.

Reason dictates and revelation commands that we must become acquainted with God's Word, for "Faith comes by hearing, and hearing by the word of God" (Romans 10:17); "Search the Scriptures" (John 5:39); "Be ready to give to every one a reason of the hope that is in you" (1 Peter 3:15). Such are the declarations and injunctions of the inspired writers — injunctions that are confirmed by those who have learned to obey these admonitions. Yet, is it not undeniable, that, with the Bible in our houses, we are ignorant of its contents; and that hence, in a great measure, the bulk of the Christian world knows so little about the Bible and is mistaken so greatly with regard to the religion they profess!

PRACTICE AND SINCERITY

This is not the place for inquiring at large why it is that those who assent to the truth that the Bible is the Word of God and who profess to rest their hopes on the Christian basis, contentedly acquiesce to a state of such lamentable ignorance. This is incomprehensible to me. However, it may not be improper here to touch on two kindred opinions from which, in the minds of the more thoughtful and serious, this acquiescence appears to derive much secret support. One of these ideas is that *it matters little what a person believes; look to his or her behavior.* A similar idea is found in this statement: *sincerity is all in all.*

It would detain us too long to set forth the various merits of these favorite positions. The former is founded altogether on that grossly fallacious assumption that a person's opinions will not influence his or her practice. The latter proceeds on this groundless supposition, that the Supreme Being has not afforded us sufficient means for discriminating truth from falsehood and right from wrong. These ideas also imply that a person's opinions or conduct, even if they are wild and extravagant, are as much the result of impartial inquiry and honest conviction, as if his sentiments and actions had been strictly conformable to the rules of reason and sobriety. Never, indeed, was there a principle more general in its use and more sovereign in its potency.

A principle like this must then be abandoned, and the advocates for sincerity must be compelled to acknowledge that it must imply honesty of mind, the faithful use of the means of knowledge and of improvement, the desire of being instructed, humble inquiry, impartial consideration, and unprejudiced judgment. It is to these I would earnestly call you. I call you to these, ever to be accompanied with fervent prayers for the divine blessing. Why? Because Scripture everywhere holds forth the most animating promises: "Ask, and ye shall receive; seek, and ye shall find; knock, and it shall be opened unto you" (Matthew 6:7); "Ho! every one that thirsteth, come ye to the waters" (Isaiah 55:1).

Such are the comfortable assurances and gracious encouragements to the truly sincere inquirer. How deep will be our guilt, if we slight all these merciful offers! How many prophets and kings have desired to hear the things that we hear and were not able to hear them! Great, indeed, are our opportunities; great, also, is our responsibility.

Therefore, let us awaken to a true sense of our situation. We have every consideration to alarm our fears and to animate our industry. How soon may the brightness of our meridian sun be darkened! Or, should the longsuffering of God still continue to give us the mercies which we so much abuse, it will only aggravate our crime, and in the end enhance our punishment. The time of reckoning will at length arrive. And when we are finally summoned to the bar of God to give an account of our stewardship, what plea can we have to urge in our defense, if we remain willingly and obstinately ignorant of the way which leads to life, with such transcendent means of knowing it, and such urgent motives to its pursuit?

Chapter Four

CORRUPTION OF HUMAN NATURE

INADEQUATE CONCEPTIONS OF THE CORRUPTION OF HUMAN NATURE

After considering the defective notions of the importance of Christianity *in general,* which prevail among nominal Christians, the particular misconceptions which first come under our notice pertain to the corruption and weakness of human nature. It is very possible that many of those into whose hands this book may fall, may not have bestowed much attention to the subject of the corruption of human nature. The subject is of the deepest import. It lies at the very root of all true religion; and, still more, it is eminently the basis and groundwork of Christianity.

Most professed Christians among the higher classes either completely overlook or deny, or at least greatly extenuate the corruption and weakness that is here in question. They acknowledge, indeed, that there is, and ever has been in the world, a great portion of vice and wickedness; likewise, they acknowledge that mankind has been ever prone to sensuality and selfishness, in disobedience to the more refined and liberal principles of their nature. Similarly, they note that in all ages and countries, both in public and in private life, innumerable instances have been afforded of oppression, rapacity, cruelty, fraud, envy, and malice. They own that it is too often in vain that you inform their understanding and convince their

53

judgment. They admit that you do not thereby reform the hearts of people. Though they know their duty, they will not practice it; no, not even when you have forced them to acknowledge that the path of virtue is that also of real interest and of solid enjoyment.

These facts are certain and they cannot be disputed; they are at the same time so obvious that one would have thought that the celebrated maxim of the Grecian sage, "The majority are wicked," would scarcely have established his claim to intellectual superiority.

But though these effects of human depravity are everywhere acknowledged and lamented, we must not expect to find them traced to their true origin. Prepare yourself to hear rather of frailty and infirmity, of petty transgressions, of occasional failings, of sudden surprises, and of such other qualifying terms as may serve to hide the true sources of the evil, and, without shocking the understanding, may administer consolation to the pride of human nature.

The bulk of professed Christians speak of human beings as being people who are naturally pure and inclined to all virtue. This is sometimes almost involuntarily drawn out of the right course or is overpowered by the violence of temptation. Vice, with them, is rather an accidental and temporary phenomenon; rather than being a constitutional and habitual distemper. A noxious plant, which, though found to live and even to thrive in the human mind, is not a natural growth and production of the soil.

Far different is the humiliating language of Christianity. From it we learn that human beings are apostate creatures, fallen from their original state, degraded in their nature, and depraved in their faculties; they are indisposed to good and disposed to evil; they are prone to vice, because it is so natural and easy for them; they are disinclined to virtue, for it is difficult and laborious to them; they are tainted with sin, not slightly and superficially, but radically, and to the very core. These are truths which, however mortifying to our pride, one would think (if this very corruption itself did not warp the judgment) none would be hardy enough to attempt to controvert it. I know of nothing which brings them home so forcibly to my own feelings, as the consideration of what still remains to us of our primitive dignity, when contrasted with our present state of moral degradation.

First, examine with attention the natural powers and faculties of humanity: our invention, reason, judgment, memory; a mind "of large discourse," "looking before and after," reviewing the past, and thence making determinations with regard to the present, and anticipating the future; discerning, collecting, combining, and comparing. We have minds that are capable not merely of apprehending, but of admiring the beauty of moral excellence with fear and hope as well as warmth and animation; with joy and sorrow to solace and soften; with love to attach; with sympathy to harmonize; with courage to attempt; with patience to endure; and with the power of conscience, that faithful monitor within our breasts, to enforce the conclusions of reason and direct and regulate the passions of the soul. Truly we must pronounce humanity as "majestic, though in ruin"! "Happy, happy world!" would be the exclamation of the inhabitant of some other planet, on being told of a globe like ours, peopled with such creatures as these, and abounding with situations and occasions to call forth the multiplied excellences of their nature.

But we have indulged too long in these delightful speculations. The sad reverse presents itself on our survey of the actual state of humanity, when, from viewing our natural powers, we look into our behavior and see the uses to which we apply them. Take in the whole of the prospect, view humanity in every age and climate and nation, in every condition and period of society. Where now do you discover the characters of the exalted nature of mankind? How is human reason clouded? How are mankind's affections perverted, and the human conscience stupefied? How do anger and envy and hatred and revenge spring up in the wretched bosom of mankind? How are humans slaves to the meanest of all appetites? What fatal propensities to evil do we discover? What inaptitude to good do we find?

Dwell awhile on the state of the ancient world—not merely on that benighted part of it in which all lay buried in brutish ignorance and barbarism, but on the seats of civilized and polished nations, on the empire of taste and learning and philosophy. Yet, in these chosen regions, with whatever luster the sun of science poured forth its rays, the moral darkness was so thick "that it might be felt." Behold their drunken idolatries, their absurd superstitions, their want of natural affection, their brutal excesses, their unfeeling oppression, their savage cruelty! Look not to the illiterate and the vulgar, but to the learned and refined. Don't form your ideas from the conduct of the less restrained and more licentious, for you will turn away with disgust and shame from the allowed and familiar habits of the decent and the moral. St. Paul best states the facts and furnishes the explanation: "Because they did not like to retain God in their knowledge, he gave them over to a reprobate mind" (Romans 1:28).

You may choose to give up the heathen nations as indefensible and wish, rather, to form your estimate of man from a view of countries which have been blessed with the light of revelation. With joy let us record the concession that Christianity has set the general tone of morals much higher than it was ever found in the pagan world. Christianity has everywhere improved the character and multiplied the comforts of society, particularly with regard to the poor and the weak, whom, from the beginning, were taken under God's patronage. Like her divine Author, "who sends his rain on the evil and on the good" (Matthew 5:45), Christianity showers down unnumbered blessings on thousands who profit from its bounty, while they forget or deny its power, and set at naught its authority. Yet, even in this more favored situation, we shall discover too many lamentable proofs of the depravity of man. Nay, this depravity will now become even more apparent and less deniable. For what bars does it not now leap over? Over what motives is it not now victorious? Consider well the superior light and advantages which we enjoy, and then appreciate the superior obligations which are imposed on us.

Consider in how many cases our evil propensities are now kept from breaking forth by the superior restraints laid upon us by positive laws and by the amended standard of public opinion. Consider, then, the superior excellence of our moral code, the new principles of obedience furnished by the Gospel, and above all the awful sanction which the doctrines and precepts of Christianity derive from the clear discovery of a future state of retribution and from the anticipation of that tremendous day "when we shall stand before the judgment-seat of Christ" (Romans 14:10). Yet, in spite of all our knowledge, thus enforced and pressed home by this solemn notice, how little has been our progress in virtue! It has been by no means such as to prevent the adoption, in our days, of various behaviors of antiquity, which, when well considered, clearly establish the depravity of man. It may not be amiss to adduce a few instances in proof of this assertion.

It is now no less acknowledged than heretofore, that prosperity hardens the heart; that unlimited power is ever abused, instead of being rendered the instrument of diffusing happiness; that habits of vice grow up of themselves, whilst those of virtue, if to be obtained at all, are of slow and difficult formation; that those who draw the finest pictures of virtue, and seem most enamored of its charms, are often the least under its influence, and by the merest trifles are drawn aside from that line of conduct which they most strongly and seriously recommend to others; that all this takes place, though most of the pleasures of vice are to be found with less alloy in the paths of virtue, while at the same time these paths afford superior and more exquisite delights, peculiar to themselves and are free from the diseases and bitter remorse, at the price of which vicious gratifications are so often purchased.

It may suffice to touch very slightly on some other arguments; one of these (the justice of which, however denied by superficial moralists, parents of strict principles can abundantly testify) may be drawn from the perverse and obstinate dispositions perceivable in children, which it is the business and sometimes the ineffectual attempt of education to reform. Another may be drawn from the various deceits we are apt to practice on ourselves, to which no one can be a stranger who has ever contemplated the operations of his own mind with serious attention. To the influence of this species of corruption it has been in a great degree owing that Christianity itself has been too often disgraced. It has been turned into an engine of cruelty, and, amidst the bitterness of persecution, every trace has disappeared of the mild and beneficent spirit of the religion of Jesus. In what degree must the taint have worked itself into the frame, and have corrupted the habit, when the most wholesome nutriment can be thus converted into the deadliest poison!

Wishing always to argue from such premises as are not only really sound, but from such as cannot even be questioned by those to whom this work is addressed, little was said in representing the deplorable state of the heathen world, respecting their defective and unworthy conceptions regarding the Supreme Being, who even then, however, "left not himself without witness, but gave them rain and fruitful seasons, filling their hearts with food and gladness."

But surely to any who call themselves Christians, it may be justly urged as an astonishing instance of human depravity, that we ourselves, who enjoy the full light of revelation – the ones to whom God has vouchsafed such clear discoveries of what it concerns us to know of His being and attributes and profess to believe "that in him we live, and move, and have our being" (Acts 17:28); that to Him we owe all the comforts we here enjoy, and the offer of eternal glory, purchased for us by the atoning blood of His own Son; "thanks be to God for his unspeakable gift" (2 Corinthians 9:15); that we, thus loaded with mercies, should, every one of us, be continually charged with forgetting His authority, and being ungrateful for His benefits; with slighting His gracious proposals, or receiving them, at best, but heartlessly and coldly.

But to put the question concerning the natural depravity of man to its severest test, take the best of the human species, the watchful, diligent, self-denying Christian, and let him or her decide the controversy; and that, not by inferences drawn from the practices of a thoughtless and dissolute world, but by an appeal to his or her personal experience. Go with him or her into his or her closet, ask him or her what his or her opinion is regarding the corruption of the heart, and he or she will tell you that he or she is deeply sensitive to its power, because he or she has learned it from much self-observation and long acquaintance with the workings of his or her own mind.

Likewise, he or she will tell you that every day strengthens this conviction, and that hourly he or she sees fresh reasons to deplore his or her want of simplicity in intention, in infirmity of purpose, in his or her low views, selfish, unworthy desires, backwardness to set about to do his or her duty, and his or her languor and coldness in performing it; that he or she finds himself or herself obliged continually to confess that he or she feels two opposite principles within, and that "he cannot do the things that he would" (Romans 7:19). He or she cries out in the language of the excellent Hooker, "The little fruit which we have in holiness, it is, God knoweth, corrupt and unsound: we put no confidence at all in it, we challenge nothing in the world for it, we dare not call God to reckoning, as if we had Him in our debt books; our continual suit to Him is, and must be, to bear with our infirmities, and pardon our offences."

Such is the moral history and such is the condition of mankind. The figures of the piece may vary, and the coloring is sometimes of a darker, sometimes of a lighter hue; but the principles of the composition, the grand outlines, are everywhere the same. Wherever we direct our view, we discover the melancholy proofs of our depravity; whether we look to ancient or modern times, to barbarous or civilized nations, to the conduct of the world around us, or to the monitor within our own breasts; whether we read, or hear, or act, or think, or feel, the same humiliating lesson is formerly drawn of the natural powers of mankind, and compare this, our actual state, with that for which, from a consideration of those powers, we seem to have been originally calculated, how are we to account for the astonishing contrast?

Will frailty or infirmity or occasional lapses or sudden surprises or any such qualifying terms convey an adequate idea of the nature or point out the cause of the distemper? How can we account for it, but by conceiving that human beings, since they came out of the hands of the Creator, have contracted a taint, and that this subtle poison has been communicated throughout the race of Adam, everywhere exhibiting incontestable marks of its fatal malignity? Hence, it has arisen that the appetites deriving new strength, and the powers of reason and conscience being weakened, the latter have feebly and impotently pleaded against those forbidden indulgences which the former have solicited. Sensual gratifications and illicit affections have debased our nobler powers and indisposed our hearts to the discovery of God and to the consideration of His perfections; to a constant, willing submission to His authority, and obedience to His laws. By a repetition of vicious acts, evil habits have been formed within us and have riveted the fetters of sin that keep us in bondage. Left to the consequences of our own folly, our human understanding has grown darker, and our hearts have become more obdurate; reason has, at length, altogether betrayed its trust, and even the conscience itself has aided that which has been forced upon us.

Such is the general account of the progress of vice, where it is suffered to attain to its full growth in the human heart. The circumstances of individuals will be found indeed to differ, but none are altogether free from its sway; all, without exception, in a greater or less degree, bear about them, more visible or more concealed, the ignominious marks of their captivity.

Such, on a full and fair investigation, must be confessed to be the state of facts; and how can this be accounted for by any other supposition than that of some original taint, some radical principle of corruption? All other solutions are unsatisfactory, while the potent cause which we have been discussing does abundantly and can alone sufficiently account for the effect. Thus, then, it appears that the corruption of human nature is proved by the same mode of reasoning as has been deemed conclusive in establishing the existence and ascertaining the laws of the principle of gravitation; that the doctrine rests on the same solid basis as the sublime philosophy of Newton; that it is not a mere speculation, and, therefore, an uncertain, though perhaps an ingenious theory, but the sure result of' a large and actual experiment, deduced from incontestable facts, and still more fully approving its truth by harmonizing with the several parts, and accounting for the various phenomena, jarring otherwise and inexplicable, of the great system of the universe.

REVELATION

Revelation, however, comes in and sustains the fallible conjectures of our unassisted reason. The holy Scriptures speak of' us as fallen creatures; on almost every page we shall find something that is calculated to abate the loftiness and silence the pretensions of man. Consider the following Scriptures: "The imagination of man's heart is evil, from his youth" (Genesis 8:21); "What is man, that he should be clean? and he which is born of a woman, that he should be righteous?" (Job 15:14); "How much more abominable and filthy is man, which drinketh iniquity like water!" (Job 15:16); "The Lord looked down from heaven upon the children of men, to see if there were any that did understand, and seek God. They are all gone aside; they are altogether become filthy: there is none that doeth good, no, not, one" (Psalm 14: 2-3); "Who can say, I have made my heart clean, I am pure from my sin?" (Proverbs 20:9). "The heart is deceitful above all things, and desperately wicked: who can know it?" (Jeremiah 17:9); "Behold, I was shapen in iniquity, and in sin did my mother conceive me" (Psalm 51:5); "O wretched man that I am! who shall deliver me from the body of this death?" (Romans 7:24).

Such passages might be multiplied upon passages, and all will speak the same language. These again might be illustrated and confirmed at large by various other considerations, drawn from the same sacred source, such as those which represent a thorough change, a renovation of our nature, as being necessary to our becoming true Christians; or as those, also, which are suggested by observing that holy men refer their good dispositions and affections to the immediate agency of the Supreme Being.

THE NATURAL STATE OF MANKIND

In addition to all which we have so far stated, the Word of God instructs us that we have to contend not only with our own natural depravity, but with the power of darkness —evil spirits and the devil—who rule in the hearts of the wicked, and whose dominion, we learn from Scripture, is so general, as to entitle Satan to be called "the prince of this world" (John 14:30). There cannot be a stronger proof of the difference which exists between the religious system of the Scriptures and that of the bulk of nominal Christians than the proof which is afforded by the subject now in question.

The existence and agency of the devil and evil spirits, though so distinctly and repeatedly affirmed in Scripture, are regarded by many as just a prejudice or a superstition, which it would now be a discredit to any man of understanding to believe. But to be consistent with ourselves, yes, we might, on the same principle, deny the reality of all other incorporeal beings.

What is there, in truth, in the doctrine, which is in itself improbable, or which is not confirmed by analogy? We see, in fact, that there are wicked people in the world—enemies of God, who are malignant towards their fellow-creatures, and who take pleasure, and often succeed, in drawing in others to the commission of evil. Why then should it be deemed incredible that there may be one or more spiritual intelligences of similar natures and propensities, who may, in like manner, be permitted to tempt men into the practice of sin?

Surely we have a retort for our opponents' charge of absurdity, and we are able to justly accuse them of gross inconsistency, in admitting, without difficulty, the existence and operation of these qualities in a material being, and yet denying them in an immaterial one, in direct contradiction to the authority of Scripture, which they allow to be conclusive, when they cannot, and will not pretend, for a moment, that there is anything belonging to the nature of matter, to which these qualities naturally adhere.

I realize that this topic may excite the ridicule of the inconsiderate and will suggest a matter of serious apprehension to all who form their opinions on the authority of the Word of God; thus, brought as we are into captivity and exposed to danger; depraved and weakened within and tempted from without, it might well fill our hearts with anxiety to reflect on the fact that the day will come when the heavens, being on fire, shall be dissolved, and the elements shall melt with fervent heat. The dead, both small and great, shall stand before the tribunal of God, and we shall have to give account of all things we've done in the body. We are naturally prompted to turn over the page of revelation with solicitude, in order to discover the qualities and character of our Judge and the probable principles of His determination; but this only serves to turn painful apprehension into fixed and certain terror!

THE QUALITIES OF OUR JUDGE

As all nature bears witness to His irresistible power, so we read in Scripture that nothing can escape His observation or elude His discovery; not our actions only, but our most secret cogitations are open to His view. "He is about our path and about our bed, and spieth out all our ways" (Psalm 139:3). "The Lord searcheth all hearts, and understandeth all the imaginations of the thoughts" (1 Chronicles 28: 9).

Now, hear His description and His character, and listen to the rule of His award: "The Lord our God is a consuming fire, even a jealous God" (Exodus 20:5); "The soul that sinneth, it shall die" (Ezekiel 18:20); "The wages of sin is death" (Romans 6:23). These strong declarations are enforced by the accounts, which, for our warning, we read in sacred history, of the terrible vengeance of the Almighty: His punishment of "the angels who kept not their first estate, and whom he hath reserved in everlasting chains, under darkness, unto the judgment of the great day" (Jude 6); the fate of Sodom and Gomorrah; the sentence issued against the idolatrous nations of Canaan, and of which the execution was assigned to the Israelites, by the express command of God, at their own peril, in the case of disobedience; the ruin of Babylon and of Tyre and of Nineveh and of Jerusalem, prophetically denounced as the punishment for their crimes and taking place in exact and terrible accordance with divine predictions. These are, indeed, matters of awful perusal, sufficient, surely, to confound the fallacious confidence of any who, on the ground that our Creator must be aware of our natural weakness, and must be of course disposed to allow for it, should allege that, though unable, indeed, to justify ourselves in the sight of God, we need not give way to such gloomy apprehensions, but might throw ourselves, with assured hope, on the infinite benevolence of the Supreme Being.

It is indeed true that along with the threats we find in the Word of God, there are mixed many gracious declarations of pardon, based on repentance and thorough amendment. But, alas, who of us is there, whose conscience must not reproach him or her with having trifled with the longsuffering of God, and with having but poorly kept the resolutions of amendment which he or she had some time or other formed in the seasons of recollection and remorse? And how is this disquietude naturally excited by such a retrospect, and is confirmed and heightened by passages like these: "Because I have called, and ye refused; I have stretched out my hand, and no man regarded; but ye have set at naught all my counsel, and would none of my reproof: I also will laugh at your calamity; I will mock when your fear cometh; when your fear cometh as desolation, and your destruction cometh as a whirlwind; when distress and anguish cometh upon you. Then shall they call upon me, but I will not answer; they shall seek me early, but they shall not find me: for that they hated knowledge, and did not choose the fear of the Lord" (Proverbs 1:24-29).

The apprehensions which must be excited by thus reading the recorded judgments and strong language of Scripture, are confirmed to the inquisitive and attentive mind by a close observation of the moral constitution of the world. We find occasion to remark that all which has been suggested of the final consequences of vice is in strict analogy to what we may observe in the ordinary course of human affairs, wherein God has established such an order of causes and effects as loudly proclaims the principles of His moral government and strongly suggests that vice and imprudence will finally terminate in misery, however interrupted here below, by hindrances and obstructions apparently of a temporary nature.

Not that this species of proof was wanted; for that which we must acknowledge on weighing the evidence to be a revelation from God requires not the aid of such a confirmation; but yet, as this accordance might be expected between the words and the works, the past and the future ordinations of the same Almighty Being, it is no idle speculation to remark that the visible constitution of things in the world around us falls in with the representations here given from Scripture, of the dreadful consequences of vice, even of what is commonly termed inconsiderateness and imprudence.

If such then be indeed our sad condition, what can be done about it? Is there no hope? Is there nothing left for us but a fearful looking for judgment and fiery indignation, which shall devour the adversaries? (See Hebrews 10:27). Blessed be God! We are not shut up irrecoverably in this sad condition. Turn to the One who is your stronghold, prisoners of hope, and hear One who proclaims His calling and His designation: " ... to heal the brokenhearted, to preach liberty to the captives, and recovering of sight to the blind" (Luke 4:18).

Those who have formed a true notion of their lost and helpless state will most gladly listen to the sound and most justly estimate the value of such a deliverance. And this is the cause, which renders it of such pressing moment not to pass cursorily over those important topics of the original and superinduced corruption and weakness of mankind; a discussion that is painful and humiliating to the pride of human nature, to which the mind lends itself with difficulty, and hearkens with a mixture of anger and disgust, but is well-suited to our case, and, like the distasteful lessons of adversity, it is permanently useful in its consequences. It is here, never let it be forgotten, that our foundation must be laid; otherwise, our superstructure, whatever we may think of it, will one day or other become insecure and start to totter.

This is, therefore, no metaphysical speculation, but a practical matter. Slight and superficial conceptions of our state of natural degradation, and of our insufficiency to recover from it of ourselves, fall in too well with our natural inconsiderateness and produce that fatal insensibility to the divine warning to flee from the wrath to come, which we cannot but observe to prevail so generally.

Having no due sense of the malignity of our disease and of its dreadful issue, we do not set ourselves to work in earnest to obtain the remedy as to a business that is arduous indeed, but indispensable; for it must ever be carefully remembered that this deliverance is not forced on us, but offered to us; we are furnished, indeed, with every help, and are always to bear in mind that we are unable, of ourselves, to will or to do rightly; but we are plainly admonished to "... work out our own salvation with fear and trembling" (Philippians 2:12). We must ever be watchful, for we are surrounded with dangers. We must be careful to put on "the whole armor of God," (Ephesians 6:11), never forgetting that we truly are beset with enemies.

May we be enabled to shake off that lethargy which is so apt to creep upon us! For this end, a deep, practical conviction of our natural depravity and weakness will be found of eminent advantage to us. It is by this that we must at first be roused from our fallacious security, so by this we must be kept wakeful and active unto the end.

Let us, therefore, make it our business to have this doctrine firmly seated in our understanding and radically worked into our hearts. With a view to the former of these objects, we should often seriously and attentively consider the firm ground on which it rests. It is plainly made known to us by the light of nature and irresistibly enforced on us by the dictates of our understanding. But, lest there should be anyone who is so obstinately dull as not to discern the force of the evidence suggested to our reason and confirmed by our experience, or rather so heedless as not to notice it, the authoritative stamp of revelation is added to complete the proof, and we must, therefore, be altogether inexcusable, if we still remain unconvinced by such an accumulated mass of argument.

We must not only assent to the doctrine clearly, but we must feel it strongly. To this end, let us accustom ourselves to refer to our natural depravity, as to its primary cause, the sad instances of vice and folly of which we read, or which we see around us, or to which we feel the propensities toward within our own bosoms.

We must be ever vigilant and distrustful of ourselves and look with an eye of kindness and pity on the faults and infirmities of others, whom we should learn to regard with the same tender concern as that with which the sick are able to sympathize with those who are suffering under the same distemper as themselves. This lesson, once it is well-acquired, will enable us to feel the benefit of it in all our future progress; and, though it be a lesson which we are slow to learn, it is one in which study and experience, the incidents of everyday living, and every fresh observation of the workings of our own hearts will gradually concur to perfect us. Let it not, after all, then, be our reproach, and, at length, our ruin, that these abundant means of instruction are possessed in vain.

THE CORRUPTION WITHIN

There is one difficulty that is more formidable than all the rest. The pride of man does not want to be humbled. Forced to abandon the plea of innocence and pressed so closely that he or she can no longer escape from the conclusion to which we would drive him or her, some bold objector, endeavors to justify what he cannot deny: "Whatever I am," he contends, "I am what my Creator made me. If this plea cannot establish my innocence, it must excuse, or at least extenuate my guilt. Frail and weak as I am, a Being of infinite justice and goodness will never try me by a rule which, however equitable in the case of creatures of a higher nature, is altogether disproportionate to mine."

Do not be alarmed by this! I am not going to enter into the discussion of the grand question concerning the origin of moral evil or attempt at large to reconcile its existence and consequent punishment with the acknowledged attributes and perfections of God. These are questions of which, if one may judge from the little success with which the acutest and profoundest people of reason have been ever laboring to solve the difficulties they contain, the full and clear comprehension is above the intellect of man. Yet, as such an objection as that which has been stated is sometimes heard from the mouths of professed Christians, it must not be passed by without a few short observations.

Were the language in question to be addressed to us by an avowed skeptic, though it might not be very difficult to expose to him or her the futility of his or her reasoning, we should almost despair of satisfying him or her with regard to the soundness of our own. We should perhaps suggest impossibilities, which might stand in the way of such a system as he or she would establish; we might, indeed, point out wherein (arguing from concessions which he or she would freely make) his or her preconceptions concerning the conduct of the Supreme Being had been, in fact, already contradicted, particularly by the existence at all of natural or moral evil, and if thus proved erroneous in one instance, why might they not be so likewise in another? But, though, by these and similar arguments, we might at length silence our objector, we could not much expect to bring him or her over to our opinions. We should probably do better, if we were to endeavor rather to draw him or her off from these dark and slippery regions and to contend with him or her on sure ground and in the light of day. Then we might fairly lay before him or her all the various arguments for the truth of our holy religion—arguments which have been sufficient to satisfy the wisest, the best, and the ablest of men.

We should afterwards, perhaps, insist on the abundant confirmation Christianity receives from its being exactly suited to the nature and wants of man; and we might conclude with fairly putting it to him or her, whether all this weight of evidence were to be overbalanced by this one difficulty, on a subject so confessedly high and mysterious, considering that we see but a part (oh, how small a part!) of the universal creation of God, and that our faculties are wholly incompetent to judge the schemes of His infinite wisdom.

This seems, at least in general, the best mode, in the case of the objection now in question of dealing with unbelievers. To adopt the contrary plan, seems somewhat like that of anyone who, having to convince some untutored person of the truth of the Copernican System, instead of beginning with plain and simple propositions, and leading him or her on to what is more abstruse and remote, should state to him or her at the outset, some astonishing problems to which the understanding can only yield its slow assent when it is constrained by the decisive force of demonstration. The novice, instead of lending himself or herself to such a mistaken method of instruction, would turn away in disgust and be only hardened against his or her tutor or headmaster.

But it must be remembered that the present work is addressed to those who acknowledge the authority of the holy Scriptures. And in order to convince all such that there is a fallacy in our objector's reasoning, it will be sufficient to establish, that though the Word of God clearly asserts the justice and goodness of the Supreme Being and also the natural depravity of man, it no less clearly lays down that this natural depravity shall never be admitted as an excuse for sin, but that " ... they which have done evil, shall rise to the resurrection of damnation" (John 5:29); "That the wicked shall be turned into hell, and all the people that forget God" (Psalm 9:17).

And it is worthy of remark, that, as if for the very purpose of more effectually silencing those unbelieving doubts which are ever springing up in the human heart, our blessed Savior, the Messenger of peace and goodwill to man, has again and again repeated these awful denunciations. Nor, it must also be remarked, are the holy Scriptures less clear and full in guarding us against supposing our sins or the dreadful consequences of them, to be chargeable to God. "Let no man say, when he is tempted, I am tempted of God: for God cannot be tempted with evil, neither tempteth he any man" (James 1:13); "The Lord is not willing that any should perish" (2 Peter 3:9). And again, where the idea is repelled as injurious to his character

"Have I any pleasure at all that the wicked should die? saith the Lord God; and not that he should return from his ways and live?" (Ezekiel 18:23); "For I have no pleasure in the death of him that dieth, saith the Lord God" (Ezekiel 18: 32). Indeed, almost every page of the Word of God contains some warning or invitation to sinners; and all these, to a considerate mind, must unquestionably be proofs of our present position.

It has been the more necessary not to leave unnoticed the objection which we have been now refuting, because, when not avowed in the daring language in which it has been above stated, it may frequently be observed in an inferior degree; and often, when not distinctly formed into shape, it lurks in secret, diffusing a general cloud of doubt or unbelief, or lowering our standard of right, or whispering fallacious comfort, and producing a ruinous tranquility.

Let us remark that, though the holy Scriptures so clearly point out the natural corruption and weakness of man, they, throughout, directly oppose the supposition that this corruption and weakness will be admitted as lowering the demands of divine justice, and in some sort palliating our transgressions of the laws of God. Such a notion is at war with the whole scheme of redemption by the Atonement of Christ. But perhaps it may be enough, when any such suggestions as those which we are condemning, force themselves into the imagination of a Christian, to recommend it to him or her to silence them by what is their best practical answer: that if our natural condition be depraved and weak, our temptations numerous, and our Almighty Judge infinitely holy; yet that the offers to penitent sinners of pardon, and grace, and strength, are universal and unlimited.

Let it not, however, surprise us if in all this there seem to be difficulties, which we cannot fully comprehend. How many of these difficulties present themselves everywhere! Scarcely is there an object around us that does not afford endless matters of doubt and argument. The meanest reptile which crawls on the Earth and every herb and flower which we behold baffle the imbecility of our limited inquiries. All nature calls upon us to be humble. Can it then be surprising if we are at a loss with regard to this question, which respects not the properties of matter or of numbers, but the counsels and ways of Him whose "understanding is infinite"? (Psalm 147:5); "Whose judgments are declared to be unsearchable, and his ways past finding out?" (Romans 11:33).

In this, our ignorance, however, we may calmly repose ourselves on His own declaration, that though "clouds and darkness are round about him, yet righteousness and judgment are the habitation of his throne" (Psalm 97:2). Let it also be remembered, that if in Christianity some things are difficult, that which it most concerns us to know is plain and obvious. To this it is true wisdom to attach ourselves, assenting to what is revealed when it is above our faculties (we do not say contradictory to them) on the credit of what is clearly discerned and satisfactorily established. In truth, we are all perhaps too apt to plunge into depths which are beyond our ability to fathom; and it was to warn us against this very error that the inspired writer, when he had been threatening the people whom God had selected as the objects of His special favor, with the most dreadful punishments, if they should forsake the Law of the Lord, and has introduced surrounding nations as asking the meaning of the severe infliction, winds up the whole with this instructive admonition: "Secret things belong unto the Lord our God; but those which are revealed belong unto us and to our children for ever, that we may do all the words of this law" (Deuteronomy 29:29).

To anyone who is seriously impressed with a sense of the critical state in which we are here placed, it is indeed an awful and an affecting spectacle to see men and women thus busying themselves in these vain speculations of arrogant curiosity and trifling with their dearest, their everlasting interests. It is but a feeble illustration of this exquisite folly, to compare it to the conduct of some convicted rebel, who, when brought into the presence of his sovereign, instead of seizing the occasion to plead for mercy, should even neglect and trifle with the pardon which should be offered to him, and insolently employ himself in prying into his sovereign's designs and criticizing his counsels. Our case, indeed, is, in another point of comparison, but too much like that of the convicted rebel. But there is this grand difference — that, at the best, his success must be uncertain; ours, if it be not our own fault, is sure: and while, on the one hand, our guilt is unspeakably greater than that of any rebel against an earthly monarch; so, on the other, we know that our Sovereign is "... longsuffering, and abundant in goodness and truth" (Exodus 34:6). The fact is that He is more ready to grant forgiveness to us than we are to ask Him for forgiveness.

Chapter Five

CHIEF DEFECTS OF THE RELIGIOUS SYSTEM / THE USE OF PASSIONS IN RELIGION

INADEQUATE CONCEPTIONS CONCERNING OUR SAVIOR AND THE HOLY SPIRIT

God so loved the world that, of His tender mercy, He gave His only Son, Jesus Christ, for our redemption. (See John 3:16.) Our blessed Lord willingly left the glory of the Father and was made man. "He was despised and rejected of men; a man of sorrows, and acquainted with grief" (Isaiah 53:3); "He was wounded for our transgressions and was bruised for our iniquities" (Isaiah 53:5). At length, He humbled himself even to the death of the cross for us, miserable sinners, so that all who, with hearty repentance and true faith, should come to Him. In doing so we shall not perish, but have everlasting life. (See John 3:16-17.)

Jesus is now at the right hand of God, making intercession for His people. (See Hebrews 7:25.) The Bible says, "Being reconciled to God by the death of his Son, we may come boldly unto the throne of grace, to obtain mercy and find grace to help in time of need" (Hebrews 4:16). Our heavenly Father will surely give His Holy Spirit to them that ask him, for the Spirit of God must dwell within us. "If any man hath not the Spirit of Christ, he is none of his" (Romans 8:9). By this divine influence, " … we are to be renewed in knowledge after the image of Him who created us" (Colossians 3:10), and "to be filled with the fruits of righteousness, to the praise of the glory of his grace" (Philippians 1:11), that, "being thus made meet for the inheritance of the saints in light" (Ephesians 1:18), we shall sleep in the Lord. Then, when the last trumpet shall sound, this corruption shall put on incorruption, and that, being at length perfected after His likeness, we shall be admitted into his Heavenly kingdom!

These are some of the leading doctrines concerning our Savior and the Holy Spirit, which are taught in the holy Scriptures and held by the Church of England. The truth of them, agreeably to our general plan, will be taken for granted. Few of those who have been used to joining in the established form of worship can have been, it is hoped, so inattentive as to be ignorant of these grand truths, which are to be found everywhere dispersed throughout our excellent liturgy.

Would to God it could be presumed with equal confidence, that all who assent to them should discern their force and excellence in their understanding, feel their power in their affections and experience their transforming influence in their hearts! What lively emotions are they calculated to excite in us, emotions of deep self-abasement and abhorrence of our sins and of humble hope, firm faith, heavenly joy, ardent love, and active, unceasing gratitude!

But here, it is to be feared, will be found the grand defect of the religion of the bulk of professed Christians — a defect like palsy in the heart, which, while in its first attack, may change but little the exterior appearance of the body, while extinguishing the internal principle of heat and motion and soon extends its benumbing influence to the remotest fibers of the frame. This defect is closely connected with that which was the chief subject of our last chapter.

Jesus said, "They that are whole need not a physician, but they that are sick" (Matthew 9:12). Had we duly felt the burden of our sins, that they are a load which our own strength is wholly unable to support, and that the weight of them must finally sink us into perdition, our hearts would have rejoiced at the sound of our Lord's gracious invitation, "Come unto me, all ye that labor and are heavy laden, and I will give you rest" (Matthew 11: 28).

But in those who have scarcely felt their sins as being any encumbrance, it would be mere affectation to pretend to very exalted conceptions of the value and acceptableness of the proffered deliverance. This pretense, accordingly, is seldom now kept up, and the most superficial observer, comparing the sentiments and views of the bulk of the Christian world with the articles still retained in their creed and with the strong language of Scripture, must be struck with the amazing disproportion that exists between the pretense and the reality.

To pass over the throng from whose minds religion is altogether excluded by the business or the vanities of life, how is it with the more decent and moral? To what criterion shall we appeal? Are their hearts really filled with these things and warmed by the love which they are adapted to inspire? Then surely their minds are apt to stray to them almost unseasonably, or at least to hasten back to them with eagerness when escaped from the estrangement imposed by the necessary cares and business of life.

"And how," someone might perhaps inquire, "do you know but that the minds of these people are thus occupied?" Let us appeal to a test to which we resorted to in a former instance: "Out of the abundance of the heart the mouth speaketh" (Matthew 12:34). Take these persons and lead the conversation to the subject of religion. The utmost which can be effected by this is to bring them to talk of things in generalities; there is nothing precise and determinate, nothing which implies a mind used to the contemplation of its object. In vain you strive to bring them to speak on that topic, which one might expect to be ever uppermost in the hearts of redeemed sinners. Nonetheless, they elude all your endeavors, and if you mention it yourself, it is received with a not very cordial welcome. Perhaps it is received with unequivocal disgust; it is, at best, a forced and formal discussion in such a case.

The excellence of our Savior's moral precepts, the kindness, simplicity, self-denial, and unblemished purity of His life, along with His patience and meekness in the hour of His death, cannot indeed be spoken of but with admiration, when spoken of at all, as they have often extorted unwilling praise from even the most daring and malignant infidels.

But are not these mentioned as qualities in the abstract, rather than as the perfections of our Patron and Benefactor and Friend, who loved us, and gave himself for us? He "... died for our offences, and rose again for our justification" (Romans 4:25), and He "... is even now at the right hand of God, making intercession for us" (Romans 8:34). Who would think that the kindness, humanity, self-denial, and patience in suffering, which we so dryly commend, had been exerted towards ourselves in acts of more than finite benevolence, of which we were to derive the benefit, in condescension and labors submitted to for our sakes, in pain and ignominy endured for our deliverance?

The Unitarians and Socinians,[1] who deny or explain away the peculiar doctrines of the Gospel, may be allowed to feel and talk of these grand truths with little emotion. But in those who profess a sincere belief in them, this coldness is insupportable. The greatest possible services of man to man must appear contemptible when they are compared with "the mercies of Christ" (Romans 12:1—mercies so dearly bought,

so freely bestowed—a deliverance from eternal misery—the
gift of "a crown of glory, that fadeth not away" (1 Peter 5:4).

A LIVELY GRATITUDE

Yet, what judgment should we form of such conduct as
is here censured, in the case of anyone who has received signal
services from a fellow-creature? True love is an ardent and
active principle. A cold, dormant, phlegmatic gratitude is a
contradiction in terms. When these generous affections really
exist in vigor, are we not ever fond of dwelling on the value
and enumerating the merits of our benefactor? How are we
moved when anything is asserted to his disparagement! How
do we delight to tell of his kindness! With what pious care
do we preserve any memorial of him, which we may happen
to possess! How gladly do we seize any opportunity of
rendering to him, or to those who are dear to him, any little
good offices, which, though in themselves of small intrinsic
worth, may testify to the sincerity of our thankfulness! The
very mention of his name will cheer the heart and enlighten
the countenance! And if he be now no more, and if he had
made it his dying request that, in a way of his own
appointment, we would occasionally meet to keep the
memory of his person and of his services in lively exercise.
How should we resent the idea of failing in the performance
of so sacred an obligation?

Such are the genuine characters and the natural workings
of a lively gratitude. And can we believe, without doing
violence to the most established principles of human nature,
that where the effects are so different, the internal principle
is in truth the same?

If the love of Christ be thus languid in the bulk of nominal
Christians, their joy and trust in Him cannot be expected to
be very vigorous. Here again we find reason to remark that

there is nothing distinct, nothing specific, nothing which implies a mind acquainted with the nature and familiarized with the use of the Christian's privileges, habitually solacing itself with the hopes held out by the Gospel.

SANCTIFICATION BY THE HOLY SPIRIT

The doctrine of the sanctifying operations of the Holy Spirit appears to have met with even worse treatment. To affirm merely that Christians are too little conscious of the inefficacy of their own unassisted endeavors after holiness of heart and life and that they are not daily employed in humbly and diligently using the appointed means for the reception and cultivation of the divine assistance is not enough. It would hardly go beyond the truth to assert, that for the most part, their notions regarding this subject are so confused and faint that they can scarcely be said to believe in the doctrine of the Holy Spirit at all.

I am prepared to hear it urged, that often where there has been the strongest pretenses to religious affections, there has been little or nothing of the reality of them; and that even omitting the instances of studied hypocrisy, what have assumed to themselves the name of religious affections have been merely the flights of a lively imagination or the working of a heated brain. That religion is of a more steady nature; and that she rejects with scorn the support of a mere feeling that is indeterminate, trivial, and useless—a feeling that varies in different people and even in the same person at different times, according to the accidental flow of the animal spirits—a feeling of which it may perhaps be said, we are, from our very nature, hardly prone towards an invisible Being.

"As to the operations of the Holy Spirit," it may probably be further urged, "it is perhaps scarcely worthwhile to spend much time in inquiring into the theory, when, in practice at least, it is manifest that there is no sure criterion whereby anyone can ascertain the reality of them, even in his own case, much less in that of another.

All we know is that pretenders to such extraordinary assistance have never been wanting to abuse the credulity of the vulgar and to try the patience of the wise. The doctrine, to say the best of it, can only serve to favor the indolence of man. It is, therefore, true wisdom to attach ourselves to what is more solid and practical—to the work of rectifying the disorders of the passions and of implanting and cultivating the virtues of the moral character.

You are contending for that which not only is altogether unworthy of our divine Master, but which, with considerate people, has ever brought His religion into suspicion and disrepute, and, under a show of honoring Him, serves only to injure and discredit His cause. Our objector, warming as he proceeds, will perhaps assume a more impatient tone. "Have not these doctrines," he may exclaim, "been ever perverted to purposes most disgraceful to the religion of Jesus? If you want an instance, look to the standard of the Inquisition, and behold the Dominicans torturing their miserable victims for the love of Christ. Or would you rather see the effects of your principles on a larger scale, and by wholesale (if the phrase may be pardoned), cast your eyes across the Atlantic, and let your zeal be edified by the 'holy activity' of Cortez and Pizarro and their counterparts in the Western Hemisphere. To what else have been owing the national persecutions and religious wars and crusades, whereby rapacity, pride, and cruelty, sheltering themselves under the mask of this specious principle, have so often afflicted the world?"

The sacred name of religion has been too often prostituted for the most detestable purposes. Furious bigots, bloody persecutors, and self-interested hypocrites, of all qualities and dimensions, have falsely called themselves Christians. These are melancholy and humiliating truths, which, as none so deeply lament them, none will more readily admit, than those who best understand the nature and are most concerned for the honor of Christianity.

We are ready to acknowledge, also, without dispute, that the doctrines of religious affections and divine assistances have almost, at all times, been more or less disgraced by the false pretenses and extravagant conduct of fanatics and enthusiasts. All this, however, is only as it happens in other instances, wherein the depravity of man perverts the bounty of God. Why is it here only to be made an argument, that there is danger of abuse? So is there, also, in the case of all the potent and operative principles, whether in the natural or moral world.

Take, for an instance, the powers and properties of matter. These were doubtless designed by Providence for our comfort and well-being; yet they are often misapplied for trifling purposes, and still more frequently turned into so many agents of misery and death. Suppose religion were discarded; then liberty remains to plague the world—a power which, though, when well-employed, the dispenser of light and happiness, has been often proved, and eminently in this very instance, to be capable, when abused, of becoming infinitely mischievous.

Well, then, extinguish liberty and blot out courage, and so might you proceed to extinguish, one by one, reason, and speech, and memory, and all the discriminating prerogatives of man. But, perhaps, more than enough has already been urged in reply to an objection so indefensible as that which would equally warrant our condemning any physical or moral faculty altogether on account of its being occasionally abused.

As to the position, that there is no way whereby the validity of pretensions to the religious affections may be ascertained, it must partly be admitted. Doubtless, we are not able always to read the hearts of people and to discover their real characters; hence, it is that we in some measure lie open to the false and hypocritical pretenses which are brought forward so triumphantly. But then these pretenses no more prove all similar claims to be founded in falsehood and hypocrisy than there having been many false and interested pretenders to wisdom and honesty would prove that there can be no such thing as a wise or an honest person. Our blessed Master himself taught us to expect as much, and when the old difficulty is stated, "Didst thou not sow good seed in thy field, whence then hath it tares?" His own answer furnishes the best solution, "An enemy hath done this."

Hypocrisy is indeed detestable, and enthusiasm sufficiently mischievous to justify our guarding against its approaches with jealous care. Yet, we are apt to draw too unfavorable conclusions from unpleasant appearances. The mode and language in which a vulgar person will express himself or herself on the subject of religion, will probably be vulgar; and it is difficult for people of literature and refinement not to be unreasonably shocked by such vulgarities. But we should at least endeavor to correct the rash judgments which we may be disposed to form on these occasions, and should learn to recognize and to prize a sound texture and just configuration, though disguised beneath homely or uncouth drapery.

PASSIONS IN RELIGION

The objection, that by insisting on the obligation of making our blessed Savior the object of our religious affections, we are degrading the worship of the understanding, and are substituting a set of mere feelings in its stead, deserves most serious consideration. If it be just, it is decisive; for ours must be unquestionably a "reasonable service" (Romans 12:1).

This notion of the affections being out of place in religion is indeed an opinion which appears to be generally prevalent. Mankind is apt to be the dupes of misapplied terms; and the progress of the persuasion now in question, has been considerably aided by an abuse of language not sufficiently checked in its first advances, whereby that species of religion which is opposite to the warm and affectionate kind, has been suffered, almost without disturbance, to usurp to itself the epithet of rational. But let not this claim be too hastily admitted. Let the position in question be thoroughly and impartially discussed, and it will appear, if I mistake not, to be a gross and pernicious error.

It cannot but afford a considerable presumption against the doctrine which we are about to combat, that it proposes to exclude at once from the service of religion, so grand a part of the composition of man; that in this, our noblest employment, it condemns, as worse than useless, all the most active and operative principles of our nature.

One cannot but suppose that, like the organs of the body, so the elementary qualities and original passions of the mind were all given to us for valuable purposes by our all-wise Creator. It is indeed one of the sad evidences of our fallen condition that they are now perpetually rebelling against the powers of reason and conscience to which they should be subject. But even if revelation had been silent, natural reason might have, in some degree, presumed that it would be the effect of a religion which should come from God, completely to repair the consequences of our super- induced depravity. The schemes of mere human wisdom had indeed tacitly confessed that this was a task beyond human strength.

Of the two most celebrated systems of philosophy, the one expressly confirmed the usurpation of the passions, while the other, despairing of being able to regulate, saw nothing left but to extinguish them. Christianity would not be driven to any such wretched expedients; it is our faith's peculiar glory and main office to bring all the faculties of our nature into their just subordination and dependence, so that the whole man, complete in all his functions, may be restored to the true ends of his being, and be devoted to the service and glory of God. To him God would say, "My son, give me thine heart, and thou shalt love the Lord thy God with all thy heart."

Such are the direct and comprehensive claims which are made on us in the holy Scriptures. We can scarcely indeed look into any part of the sacred volume without meeting abundant proofs that it is the religion of the affections which God particularly requires. Love, zeal, gratitude, joy, hope, trust—each of them is specified, and they are not allowed to be as weaknesses to us, but they are enjoined on us as our bounden duty and are commended to us as our acceptable worship. Where passages are so numerous, there would be no end of particular citations. Let it be sufficient, therefore, to refer the reader to the Word of God. There I want you to observe, too, that as the lively exercise of the passions towards their legitimate object is always spoken of with praise, so a cold, hard, unfeeling heart is represented as being highly criminal.

Lukewarmness is stated to be the object of God's disgust and aversion; zeal and love, on the other hand, are the objects of His favor and delight. The taking away of the heart of stone, and the implanting of a warmer and more tender nature in its stead is specifically promised as the effect of His returning favor and the work of His renewing grace.

It is the prayer of an inspired Teacher in behalf of those for whom He was most interested, "that their love" (already acknowledged to be to the most eminent of the Scripture characteristics) will make them warm, zealous, and affectionate. When engaged in their favorite work of celebrating the goodness of their Supreme Benefactor, their souls appear to burn within them, and their hearts kindle into rapture.

The powers of language are inadequate to express these feelings, and they call on all nature to unite with them in hallelujahs of gratitude, joy, and praise. The person after God's own heart most of all abounds in these glowing effusions, and His compositions appear to have been given to us in order to set the tone, as it were, to all succeeding generations. Accordingly (to quote the words of a late excellent prelate, who was himself warmed with the same heavenly flame), "In the language of this divine Book, the praises of the Church have been offered up to the throne of grace from age to age."

Again, when it pleased God to check the future apostle of the Gentiles (Paul) in his wild career, and to make him a monument of transforming grace, was the force of his affections diminished, or was it not only that their direction was changed? He brought his affections entire and unabated into the service of his blessed Master. His zeal now burned even with an increase of brightness and no intenseness, no continuance of suffering, could allay its ardor or dampen the fervors of his triumphant exultations.

Finally, the worship and service of the glorified spirits in Heaven is not represented to us as a cold, intellectual experience. Those modes of worship are set forth and prescribed, which are best calculated to excite the dormant affections and to maintain them in lively exercise. They form the worship and service of gratitude and love. And surely it will not be disputed that it should be, even here, the humble endeavor of those who are promised, while on earth "to be made meet to be partakers of the inheritance of the saints in light" (Colossians 1:12), in order to bring their hearts into a capacity for joining in those everlasting praises.

But it may be advisable here to guard against a mistaken
supposition, that the force of the religious affections is to be
mainly estimated by the degree of mere animal fervor, by
ardors, and transports, and rapture, of which, from a
constitutional temperament, a person may be easily
susceptible; or into which daily experience must convince us
that people of strong conceptions and of warm passions may
work themselves without much difficulty, where their hearts
are by no means truly or deeply interested.

These high degrees of the passions bad men may
experience, and good men may want. They may be affected;
they may be genuine; but, whether genuine or affected, they
form not the true standard by which the real nature or
strength of the religious affections is to be determined. To
ascertain these points, we must examine whether they appear
to be grounded in knowledge, to have their root in strong
and just conceptions of the great, manifold excellences of
their objects, or to be ignorant, unmeaning, or vague; we
must discover whether they are natural and easy, or
constrained and forced; wakeful and apt to fix on their great
objects, delighting in their proper nutriment, the exercises of
prayer and praise, and religious contemplation; or voluntarily
omitting offered occasions of receiving it, looking forward
to them with little expectation, looking back on them with
little complacency, and being disappointed in them with little
regret.

We must observe whether these religious affections are
merely occasional visitants, or the abiding inmates of the
soul—whether they have the mastery over the vicious passions
and propensities, with which, in their origin, nature, and
tendency, they are at open variance; or whether, if the victory
be not yet complete, the war is at least constant, and the
breach irreconcilable.

We must observe whether they moderate and regulate all the inferior appetites and desires, which are culpable only in their excess, thus striving to reign in the bosom with a settled, undisputed predominance. We must examine whether, above all, they manifest themselves by prompting us to the active discharge of the duties of life: the personal, the domestic, the relative, the professional, and social and civil duties. Here the wideness of their range and the universality of their influence will generally distinguish them from those partial efforts of diligence and self-denial to which mankind is prompted by subordinate motives. All proofs, other than those deduced from conduct, are in some degree ambiguous. This, whether we argue from reason or from Scripture, is a sure, infallible criterion.

THE PASSION OF LOVE

From the daily incidents of conjugal and domestic life, we learn that a warmth of affection, occasionally vehement, but superficial and transitory, may consist of a course of conduct exhibiting incontestable proofs of neglect and unkindness. But the passion, which alone the holy Scriptures dignify with the name of love, is a deep, not superficial feeling; it is a fixed and permanent condition, not an occasional emotion. It proves the validity of its title by actions corresponding with its nature, by practical endeavors to gratify the wishes and to promote the interests of the object of affection.

Jesus said, "If a man loves me, he will keep my sayings" (John 14:15), and John wrote, "This is the love of God, that we keep his commandments" (1 John 5:3). Love, therefore, is the best standard by which to try the quality or to ascertain the quality, and to estimate the strength of the religious affections. Without suffering ourselves to derive too much complacency from transient fervors of devotion, we should carefully and frequently prove ourselves by this more accurate test — by impartially examining our daily conduct; and often comparing our actual with our possible services. We must look closely at the fair amount of our exertions with our natural or acquired means and opportunities of usefulness.

We are perfectly ready to concede to the objector, whose arguments we have so long been considering, that the religious affections must be expected to be more or less lively in different people, and in the same person at different times, in proportion to natural tempers, ages, situations, and habits of life. But to found an objection on this ground, would be as unreasonable as it would altogether be to deny the obligation of the precepts which command us to relieve the necessities of the indigent, because the infinitely varying circumstances of mankind must render it impossible to specify, beforehand, the sum which each individual ought, on the whole, to allot to this purpose, or to fix, in every particular instance, on any determinate measure and mode of contribution.

In the one case, no less than in the other, we may apply the maxim of an eminent writer; "An honest heart is the best casuist." He who everywhere but in religion is warm and animated, and there only phlegmatic and cold, can hardly expect (especially if this coldness be not the subject of unfeigned humiliation and sorrow), that his plea on the ground of natural temper should be admitted any more than that of a person who should urge his poverty as a justification of his not relieving the wants of the needy, at the very time when he should be launching out into expense without restraint, on occasions in which he should be really prompted by his inclinations. In both cases, "Every man will be judged according to what he hath, and not according to what he hath not" (2 Corinthians 8:12).

After the decisive proofs that we have already adduced from the Word of God, of the unreasonableness of the objection to the admission of the passions into religion, all further arguments may appear superfluous to anyone who is disposed to bow to scriptural authority. Yet, the point is of so much importance, and, it is so little regarded, that it may not be wrong to continue the discussion.

The best results of our understanding will be shown to fall in with what clearly appears to be the authoritative language of revelation, and to call in the aid of the affections to the service of religion will prove to be not only what sober reason may permit, but to be that which she clearly and strongly dictates to our deliberate judgments, as being what the circumstances of our natural condition indispensably requires.

PERSEVERANCE

Each of us has a work to accomplish, wherein our eternal interests are at stake—a work to which we are naturally indisposed. We live in a world abounding with objects which distract our attention and divert our endeavors, and a deadly enemy is ever at hand to seduce and beguile us. If we persevere, indeed, success is certain; but our efforts must know no remission. There is a call on our lives for vigorous and continual resolution, self-denial, and activity. So, we see that human beings are not simply beings of mere intellect.

Video meliora proboque, deteriora sequor[2]—is a complaint which, alas, we all might daily utter. The slightest solicitation of appetite is often able to draw us to act in opposition to our clearest judgment, our highest interests, and most resolute determinations. Sickness, poverty, disgrace, and even eternal misery itself, sometimes in vain solicit our regards; they are all excluded from the view, and thrust, as it were, beyond the sphere of vision, by some poor, unsubstantial, transient object, so minute and contemptible as to almost escape the notice of the eye of reason.

These observations are more strikingly confirmed in our religious concerns than in any other arena, because in them the interests at stake are of transcendent importance. They hold equally in every instance, according to its measure, wherein there is a call for laborious, painful, and continued exertions, from which anyone is likely to be deterred by obstacles or seduced by the solicitations of pleasure.

What, then, is to be done in the case of any such arduous and necessary undertaking? The answer is obvious: You should endeavor not only to convince your understanding, but also to affect your heart; and to this end, you must secure the reinforcement of your passions. This is indeed the course which would be naturally followed by every person of common understanding, who should know that someone for whom he or she was deeply interested, a child, for instance, or a brother, were about to enter on a long, difficult, perilous, and critical adventure, wherein success would be honor and affluence, and defeat would be contempt and ruin. And still more, if the parent were convinced that his or her child possessed faculties which, strenuously and unremittingly exerted, would prove equal to all the exigencies of the enterprise, but knew him or her also to be volatile and inconstant, and had reason to doubt his resolution and his vigilance, how would the friendly monitor's endeavor be redoubled, so as to possess his or her pupil's mind with the worth and dignity of the undertaking, that there should be no opening for the entrance of any inferior consideration? "Weigh well," he would say, "the value of the object for which you are about to contend, and contemplate and study its various excellencies, till your whole soul is on fire for its acquisition.

"Consider, too, that, if you fail, misery and infamy are united in the alternative which awaits you. Let not the mistaken notion of its being a safe and easy service beguile you for a moment into the discontinuance or remission of your efforts. Be aware of your imminent danger, and at the same time know your true security. It is a service of labor and peril; but one wherein the powers which you possess, strenuously and perseveringly exerted, cannot but crown you with victory. Accustom yourself to look first to the dreadful consequences of failure; then fix your eye on the glorious prize which is before you; and when your strength begins to fail, and your spirits are nearly exhausted, let the animating view rekindle your resolution, and call forth in renewed vigor the fainting energies of your soul."

This is the remark of an unerring observer, "The children of this world are wiser in their generation than the children of light." And it is indisputably true, that in religion we have to argue and plead with men for principles of action, the wisdom and expediency of which are universally acknowledged in matters of worldly concern.

So it is in the instance before us. The case which has been just described is an exact but faint representation of our condition in this life. Frail and "infirm of purpose," we have a business to execute of supreme and indispensable necessity. Solicitations to neglect it abound everywhere. The difficulties and dangers are numerous and urgent, and the night of death cometh. How soon it will come, we do not know, but we do know that it is the time "when no man can work." All this is granted.

This seems to be a state of things wherein one should look out with solicitude for some powerful stimulants. Mere knowledge is confessedly too weak. The affections alone are there to supply the deficiency. They precisely meet the occasion and suit the purposes intended. Yet, when we

propose to fit ourselves for our great undertaking, by calling
them in to help us, we are to be told that we are acting
contrary to reason. Is this reasonable, to strip us first of our
armor of proof, and then to send us to the sharpest of
encounters? To summon us to the severest labors, but first
to rob us of the precious cordials which should brace our
sinews and recruit our strength?

Let these pretended advocates for reason then confess
their folly and do justice to the superior wisdom as well as
goodness of our heavenly Instructor, who, better
understanding our true condition and knowing our
forwardness and inadvertency, has most reasonably, as well
as kindly pointed out and enjoined on us the use of those
aids which may counteract our infirmities, and who,
commanding the effect, has commanded also the means
whereby it may be accomplished.

And now, if the use of the affections in religion, in general,
be at length shown to be conformable to reason, it will not
require many words to prove that our blessed Savior is the
proper object of them. We know that love, gratitude, joy,
hope, trust (the affections in question), all have their
appropriate objects.

Now it must be at once conceded, that if these appropriate
objects be not exhibited, it is perfectly unreasonable to expect
that the correspondent passions should be excited. If we ask
for love, in the case of an object which has no excellence or
desirableness; for gratitude, where no obligation has been
conferred; for joy, where there is no just cause of self-
congratulation; for hope, where nothing is expected; for trust,
where there exists no ground of reliance; then, indeed, we
must kiss the rod, and patiently submit to correction. This
would be indeed Egyptian bondage, to demand the effects
without the means of producing them. Is the case then so?

Are we ready to adopt the language of the avowed enemies of our adorable Savior and again to say of Him "in whom dwelleth all the fullness of the Godhead bodily" (Colossians 2:9), that "He hath no form nor comeliness; and when we shall see him, there is no beauty that we should desire him?" (Isaiah 53:2). Is it no obligation that he who "thought it not robbery to be equal with God" (Philippians 2:6), should yet, for our sakes, "make himself of no reputation, and take upon him the form of a servant, and be made in the likeness of men; and humble himself, and become obedient unto death, even the death of the cross?" (Philippians 2:6-8).

Is it no cause of "joy, that to us is born a Savior" (Luke 2:10-11), by whom we may "be delivered from the power of darkness, and be made meet to be partakers of the inheritance of the saints in light" (Colossians 1:12-13)? Can there be a "hope comparable to that of our calling" (Ephesians 1:18), "which is Christ in us, the hope of glory" (Colossians 1: 27)? Can there be a trust to be preferred to the reliance on "Christ Jesus, who is the same yesterday, today, and for ever" (Hebrews 13:8). Surely, if our opponent be not dead to every generous emotion, he cannot look his own objection in the face without a blush of shame and indignation.

REASONABLE AFFECTIONS TOWARD GOD

Forced at last to retreat from his favorite position, and compelled to acknowledge that the religious affections towards our blessed Savior are not unreasonable; he still, however, maintains the combat, suggesting that, by the very constitution of our nature, we are not susceptible to them towards an invisible Being; in whose case, it will be added, we are shut out from all those means of communication and intercourse which knit and cement the union between man and man.

Pure Gold Classics

CHRISTIAN CLASSICS

A classic is a work of enduring excellence; a Christian classic is a work of enduring excellence that is filled with divine wisdom, biblical revelation, and insights that are relevant to living a godly life. Such works are both spiritual and practical. Our Pure Gold Classics contain some of the finest examples of Christian writing that have ever been published, including the works of John Foxe, Charles Spurgeon, D.L. Moody, Martin Luther, John Calvin, Saint John of the Cross, E.M. Bounds, John Wesley, Andrew Murray, Hannah Whitall Smith, and many others.

The timeline on the following pages will help you to understand the context of the times in which these extraordinary books were written and the historical events that must have served to influence these great writers to create works that will always stand the test of time. Inspired by God, many of these authors did their work in difficult times and during periods of history that were not sympathetic to their message. Some even had to endure great persecution, misunderstanding, imprisonment, and martyrdom as a direct result of their writing.

The entries that are printed in green type will give you a good overview of Christian history from the birth of Jesus to modern times.

The entries in red pertain to writers of Christian classics from Saint Augustine, who wrote his *Confessions* and *City of God*, to Charles Sheldon, twentieth-century author of *In His Steps*.

Entries in black provide a clear perspective on the development of secular history from the early days of Buddhism (first century) through the Civil Rights Movement.

Finally, the blue entries highlight secular writers and artists, including Chaucer, Michelangelo, and others.

Our color timeline will provide you with a fresh perspective of history, both secular and Christian, and the classics, both secular and Christian. This perspective will help you to understand each author better and to see the world through his or her eyes.

1714-1770 George Whitefield, Calvinist evangelist known for powerful preaching and revivals in England and America. Friend of John Wesley.

1720-1760 "The Great Awakening" in America. Numerous revivals result in widespread Church growth.

1741 Handel's *Messiah* composed.

1756-1763 Seven Years War in Europe, Britain defeats France.

1759-1833 William Wilberforce, British abolitionist and author of *A Practical View of Christianity*.

1775-1783 American Revolutionary War.

1779 Olney Hymns published, John Newton's *Amazing Grace*.

1789 French Revolution begins.

1792-1875 Charles Finney, American evangelist. Leads Second Great Awakening in 1824.

1805-1898 George Mueller, English evangelist & founder of orphanages; author, *Answers to Prayer*.

1813-1855 Soren Kierkegaard, Danish philosopher & theologian; author, *Fear and Trembling*.

1816-1900 J.C. Ryle, author of *Practical Religion* and *Holiness*.

1820-1915 "Fanny" Crosby, though blind, pens over 8,000 hymns.

1828-1917 Andrew Murray, author of *Humility, Abide in Christ, With Christ in the School of Prayer,* and *Absolute Surrender*.

1828 Noah Webster publishes a dictionary of the English Language.

1829 Salvation Army founded by William and Catherine Booth.

1832-1911 Hannah Whitall Smith, author of *The Christian's Secret to a Happy Life* and *God of All Comfort*.

1834-1892 Charles H. Spurgeon, author of *Morning by Morning* and *The Treasury of David*.

1835-1913 E.M. Bounds, author of *The Classic Collection on Prayer*.

1836-1895 A.J. Gordon, New England Spirit-filled pastor; author, *The Ministry of the Spirit*.

1837-1899 Dwight L. Moody, evangelist and founder of Moody Bible Institute in Chicago. Author of *Secret Power* and *The Way to God*.

1843-1919 A.B. Simpson, founder of Christian and Missionary Alliance, author of *The Fourfold Gospel*.

1844 Samuel Frank Morse invents the telegraph.

1847-1929 F.B. Meyer, English Baptist pastor & evangelist; author, *Secret of Guidance*.

1857-1858 Third Great Awakening in America; Prayer Meeting Revival.

1851-1897 Henry Drummond, author of *The Greatest Thing in the World … Love*.

1856-1928 R.A. Torrey, American evangelist, pastor and author.

1857-1946 Charles Sheldon, author of *In His Steps*.

1859 Theory of evolution; Charles Darwin's *Origin of Species*.

1861-1865 American Civil War.

1862-1935 Billy Sunday, American baseball player who became one of the most influential evangelists in the 20th century. *Collected Sermons*.

1867 Alexander Graham Bell invents the telephone.

1869-1948 Mahatma Gandhi makes his life's work India's peaceful independence from Britain.

1881-1936 J. Gresham Machen, "Old School" Presbyterian leader, writes *Christianity and Liberalism*; forms the new Orthodox Presbyterian Church in 1936.

1886-1952 A. W. Pink, evangelist & biblical scholar; author, *The Sovereignty of God*.

1897-1963 A.W. Tozer, author of *Fellowship of the Burning Heart*.

1898-1900 Boxer Rebellion in China deposes western influence, particularly Christian missionaries.

c. 1900-1930 *The Kneeling Christian* (Written by The Unknown Christian.)

1901 American Standard Version of Bible published.

1906 Azusa Street Revival, Los Angeles, instrumental in rise of modern Pentecostal Movement.

1906-1945 Dietrich Bonhoeffer spreads Christian faith to Germans in opposition to WWII Nazism.

1914-1918 World War I.

1917 Bolshevik Revolution in Russia.

1925 Scopes Monkey Trial pits Bible against theory of evolution.

1929 US Stock Market crashes, 12 years of Great Depression.

1939-1945 World War II. Holocaust in eastern Europe under Hitler.

1947 Dead Sea Scrolls found in caves in Judean desert.

1948 State of Israel reestablished.

1949 Communist revolution in China; religion suppressed.

1952 RSV Bible first published.

1960s Civil Rights movement in the United States.

We mean not to deny that there is something in this objection. It might even seem to plead the authority of Scripture in its favor: "He that loveth not his brother whom he hath seen, how can he love God whom he hath not seen?" (1 John 4:20).

We receive impressions more readily from visible objects, we feel them more strongly, and retain them more durably. But though it must be granted that this circumstance makes it a more difficult task to preserve the affections in question in a healthful and vigorous state, is it thereby rendered impossible? This were indeed a most precipitate conclusion to make; and anyone who should be disposed to admit the truth of it, might at least hesitate, when he or she should reflect that the argument applies equally against the possibility of the love of God, a duty of which the most cursory reader of Scripture, if he or she admits its divine authority, cannot but acknowledge the indispensable obligation. But we need only look back to the Scripture proofs which have been lately adduced, to be convinced that the religious affections are therein inculcated within us as a matter of high and serious obligation.

If the principles of love—gratitude, joy, hope, and trust —are not utterly extinct within us, they cannot but be called forth by the various corresponding objects which the contemplation of our blessed Redeemer would gradually bring forth to our view. Well might the language of the apostle be addressed to Christians, "Whom having not seen, ye love; in whom, though now ye see him not, yet believing, ye rejoice with joy unspeakable and fall of glory" (1 Peter 1:8).

Our blessed Savior, if we may be permitted to say so, is not removed far from us; and the various relations in which we stand towards Him seem purposely made known to us in order to furnish so many different bonds of connection with Him and consequent occasions of continual intercourse. He exhibits not himself to us "dark with excessive brightness,"

95

but is let down, as it were, to the possibilities of human converse.

We may not think that He is incapable of entering into our little concerns and sympathizing with them, for we are graciously assured that He is not one "who cannot be touched with the feeling of our infirmities, having been in all points tempted like as we are" (Hebrews 4:15).

The figures by which He is represented in the Bible convey ideas of the utmost tenderness. "He shall feed his flock like a shepherd; he shall gather the lambs in his arm, and carry them in his bosom, and shall gently lead those that are with young" (Isaiah 40:11). "They shall not hunger nor thirst, neither shall the heat nor sun smite them; for he that hath mercy on them shall lead them, even by the springs of water shall he guide them" (Isaiah 49:10). "I will not leave you orphans,"[3] was one of his last consolatory declarations. (See John 14:18.)

The children of Christ are here separated indeed from the personal view of Him; but not from His paternal affection and paternal care. Meanwhile, let them quicken their regards by the animating anticipation of that blessed day, when He "who is gone to prepare a place for them, will come again to receive them unto himself" (John 14:2). Then shall they be admitted into His more immediate presence: "Now we see through a glass, darkly; but then face to face: now I know in part; but then shall I know even as also I am known" (1 Corinthians 13:12).

Surely more than enough has been said to prove that this particular case, from its very nature, furnishes the most abundant and powerful considerations and means for exciting the feelings; and it might be contended, without fear of refutation, that by the diligent and habitual use of those considerations and means, we might, with confident expectation of success, engage in the work of raising our affections towards our blessed Savior to a state of due force and activity.

But, blessed be God, we have a still better reliance; for the grand circumstance of all yet remains behind, which I have been led to defer because of my wish to contend with my opponents on their own ground. This circumstance is, that here, no less than in other particulars, the Christian's hope is founded, not on the speculations or the strength of mankind, but on the declaration of Him who cannot lie— on the power of Omnipotence.

We learn from the Scriptures that it is one main part of the operations of the Holy Spirit to implant these heavenly principles within the human mind, and to nurture their growth. We are encouraged to believe that, in answer to our prayers, this aid from above will give efficacy to our earnest endeavors when it is used in humble dependence on divine grace.

We may, therefore, with confidence, take the means which have been suggested. But let us, in our turn, be permitted to ask our opponents this question: have they humbly and perseveringly applied for this divine strength? Or, disclaiming that assistance, perhaps as tempting them to indolence, have they been so much the more strenuous and unwearied in the use of their own unaided endeavors? Or, rather, have they not been equally negligent of both? Renouncing the one, they have wholly omitted the other. But this is far from being all. They even reverse all the methods which we have recommended as being calculated to increase regard, and exactly follow that course which would be pursued by anyone who should wish to reduce an excessive affection.

Yet, thus leaving untried all the means which, whether from reason or Scripture, we maintain to be necessary to the production of the end, nay, using such as are of a directly opposite nature, these men presume to talk to us of impossibilities! We may rather contend that they furnish a fresh proof of the soundness of our reasoning. We lay it down as a fundamental position, that speculative knowledge alone, that mere superficial, cursory considerations, will be of no avail. Nothing is to be done without the diligent, continued use of the appointed method. They themselves afford an instance of the truth of our assertions; and while they supply no argument against the efficacy of the mode prescribed, they acknowledge at least that they are wholly ignorant of any other.

TRUE CHRISTIANS

But let us now turn our eyes to Christians of a higher order, to those who have actually proved the truth of our reasoning, those who have not only assumed the name, but who have possessed the substance and felt the power of Christianity, who, though often foiled by their remaining corruptions, and shamed and cast down under a sense of their many imperfections, have known in their better seasons what it was to experience its firm hope, its dignified joy, its unshaken trust, its more-than-human consolations. In their hearts, love also towards their Redeemer has glowed—a love not superficial and unmeaning (think not that this would be the subject of our praise)—but constant and rational, resulting from a strong impression of the worth of its object and heightened by an abiding sense of great, unmerited, and continually accumulating obligations—ever manifesting itself in acts of diligent obedience or of patient suffering. Such was the religion of the holy martyrs of the sixteenth century, the illustrious ornaments of the Christian Church. They realized the theory which we have now been faintly tracing. Look to their writings, and you will find that their thoughts and affections had been much exercised in habitual views of the blessed Jesus.

Thus, they used the required means. What were the effects? Persecution, distress, degradation, and contempt assailed them in vain; all these evils served but to bring their affections into closer contact with their object; and not only did their love feel no diminution or abatement, but it rose to all the exigencies of the occasion and burned with an increase of ardor. And when they were taken at last to a cruel and ignominious death, they repined not at their fate, but rather rejoiced that they were counted worthy to suffer for the name of Christ.

By the blessing of God I might refer to still more recent times. But lest His authorities should be disputed, let us go to the apostles of our Lord, and while, on a very cursory perusal of their writings, we must acknowledge that they commend and even prescribe to us the love of Christ, as one of the chief of the Christian graces, so, on a more attentive inspection of those writings, we shall discover abundant proofs that they were themselves bright examples of their own precepts—that our blessed Savior was really the object of their warmest affection, and what He had done and suffered for them became the continual matter of their grateful remembrance.

The disposition so prevalent in the bulk of nominal Christians, to form a religious system for themselves instead of taking it from the Word of God, is strikingly observable in their scarcely admitting, except in the most vague and general sense, the doctrine of the influences of the Holy Spirit. If we took into the Scriptures for information on this particular, we learn a very different lesson. We are distinctly taught, that "of ourselves we can do nothing" and that "we are by nature children of wrath" who are under the power of the enemy We further learn that our understanding is naturally dark, and our hearts are averse toward spiritual things. We are directed to pray for the influences of the Holy

Spirit to enlighten our understandings, to dissipate our prejudices, to purify our corrupt minds, and to renew us after the mind of our heavenly Father.

It is this influence which is represented as originally awakening us from slumber and as enlightening us in darkness, as "quickening us when we were dead" (Ephesians 2:1-5), as "delivering us from the power of the devil," as drawing us to God, as "translating us into the kingdom of his dear Son" (Colossians 1:13), as creating us anew in Christ Jesus" (Ephesians 2:10), as "dwelling in us, and walking in us" (2 Corinthians 6:16), so that "putting off the old man with his deeds," we are to consider ourselves as "having put on the new man, which is renewed in knowledge after the image of Him that created him" (Colossians 3:9-10), and as those who are to be "an habitation of God through the Spirit" (Ephesians 2:22). It is by this divine assistance only that we can grow in grace and improve in all holiness.

So expressly, particularly, and repeatedly does the Word of God inculcate these lessons within us, that one would think there were scarcely room for any difference of opinion among those who admit to the Bible's authority. Sometimes[4] the whole of a Christian's repentance and faith, and consequent holiness, are ascribed generally to the divine influence; sometimes these are spoken of separately and ascribed to the same Almighty power. Sometimes different, particular graces of the Christian character, those which respect our duties and tempers towards our fellow-creatures, no less than those which have reference to the Supreme Being, are particularly traced to this source. Sometimes they are all traced collectively to this common root, being comprehended under "the fruits of the Spirit." (Galatians 5:22-23). In exact correspondence with these representations, this aid from above is promised in other parts of Scripture, as well, for the production of those effects; and the withholding or

withdrawing of it is occasionally threatened as a punishment
for the sins of men and as one of the most fatal consequences
of the divine displeasure.

BEING ACCEPTED BY GOD

If, then, it be indeed as I have now stated—that, in
contradiction to the plainest dictates of Scripture, the
sanctifying operations of the Holy Spirit, the first fruits of
our reconciliation to God, the purchase of our Redeemer's
death, and His best gift to His true disciples are too generally
undervalued and slighted; if it be also true, as was formerly
proved, that our thoughts of the blessed Savior are confused
and faint and our affections towards Him languid and
lukewarm, little proportioned to what those who at such a
price have been rescued from ruin, and endowed with a title
to eternal glory, might be justly expected to feel towards the
Author of their deliverance, little proportioned to what has
been felt by others, ransomed from the same ruin, and
partakers of the same inheritance—if this, let it be repeated,
be indeed so, let us not shut our eyes against the perception
of our real state, but, rather, endeavor to trace the evil to its
source.

We are loudly called on to examine well our foundations.
If there is anything found there that is unsound and hollow,
the superstructure could not be safe, though its exterior were
less suspicious. Let the question then be asked, and let the
answer be returned with all the consideration and solemnity
which a question so important may justly demand, whether,
in the grand concern of all, the means of a sinner's acceptance
with God, there is not reason to apprehend, that the nominal
Christians whom we have been addressing, too generally
entertain very superficial, confused, and (to speak in the
softest terms) highly dangerous notions?

Is there not reason to fear, that with little more than an indistinct and nominal reference to Him who "bore our sins in his own body on the tree," they really rest their eternal hopes on a vague, general persuasion of the unqualified mercy of the Supreme Being; or that, still more erroneously, they rely in the main on their own negative or positive merits?

They can look upon their lives with an impartial eye, and congratulate themselves on their inoffensiveness in society; on their having been exempt at least from any gross vice, or if sometimes accidentally betrayed into it, on its never having been indulged in habitually. Or if not even so (for there are but few who can say this, if the term vice be explained according to the strict requisitions of the Gospel), yet on the balance being in their favor, or, on the whole, not much against them, when their good and bad actions are fairly weighed and due allowance is made for human frailty.

These considerations are sufficient for the most part to compose their apprehensions; these are the cordials which they find most at hand in the moments of serious thought, or of occasional dejection; and sometimes, perhaps, in seasons of less-than-ordinary self-complacency, they call in also to their aid, the general persuasion of the unbounded mercy and pity of God.

Yet persons of this description by no means disclaim a Savior, or avowedly relinquish their title to a share in the benefits of His death. They close their petitions with the name of Christ; but if not chiefly from the effect of habit, or out of decent conformity to the established faith, yet surely with something of the same ambiguity of principle which influenced the expiring philosopher, when he ordered the customary mark of homage to be paid to the god of medicine.

Others go farther than this; for there are many shades of difference between those who flatly renounce and those who cordially embrace the doctrine of redemption by Christ. This class has a sort of general, indeterminate, and poorly understood dependence on our blessed Savior. But their hopes, so far as they can be distinctly made out (for their views also are very obscure), appear ultimately to be founded on the persuasion that they have now, through Christ, become members of a new dispensation, wherein they will be tried by a more lenient rule than that to which they must have been otherwise subject. Their reasoning is this: "God will not now be extreme to mark what is done amiss, but He will dispense with the rigorous exactions of His law, too strict, indeed, for such frail creatures as we are to hope that we can fulfill it.

In their minds Christianity has moderated the requisitions of divine justice; and all which is now required of us is thankfully to trust to the merits of Christ for the pardon of our sins and the acceptance of our sincere, though imperfect obedience. The frailties and infirmities to which our nature is liable, or to which our situation in life exposes us, will not be severely judged; and, as it is practice that really determines the character, we may rest satisfied, that if, on the whole, our lives are tolerably good, we shall escape with little or no punishment, and, through Jesus Christ our Lord, shall be finally partakers of heavenly felicity.

We cannot dive into the human heart, and, therefore, should always speak with caution and diffidence when, from external appearances or declarations, we are affirming the existence of any internal principles and feelings, especially as we are liable to be misled by the ambiguities of language or by the inaccuracy with which others may express themselves. But it is sometimes not difficult to anyone who is accustomed (if the phrase may be allowed) to the anatomy of the human mind, to discern, that generally speaking, the persons who use the above language rely not so much on the merits of Christ and on the agency of divine grace, as on their own power of fulfilling the moderated requisitions of divine justice. Such a person will hence, therefore, discover within himself or herself a disposition rather to extenuate the malignity of their disease than to magnify the excellence of the proffered remedy. He or she will find them apt to palliate in himself or herself what he or she cannot fully justify, to enhance the merit of what he or she believes to be his or her good qualities and commendable actions, to set, as it were, in an account the good against the bad; and if the result be not very unfavorable, he or she conceives that he or she shall be entitled to claim the benefits of our Savior's sufferings as a thing of course.

They have little idea, so little, that it might almost be affirmed that they have no idea at all, of the importance or difficulty of the duty of what the Scripture calls "submitting ourselves to the righteousness of God;" or of our proneness rather to justify ourselves in His sight, than in the language of imploring penitents to acknowledge ourselves as being guilty and helpless sinners.

They have never summoned themselves to this entire and unqualified renunciation of their own merits and their own strength; and, therefore, they remain strangers to the natural loftiness of the human heart, which such a call would have awakened into action and roused to resistance. Their several errors naturally result from the mistaken conception entertained of the fundamental principles of Christianity. They consider not that Christianity is a method for "justifying the ungodly" (Romans 4:5), by Christ's dying for them "when yet sinners"[5] (Romans 5:6-8). This is the divine plan "for reconciling us to God, when we were His enemies," and for making the fruits of holiness the effects, not the cause, of their being justified and reconciled; that, in short, it opens freely the door of mercy to the greatest and vilest of penitent sinners; that obeying the blessed impulse of the grace of God, whereby they had been awakened from the sleep of death, and moved to seek for pardon, they might enter in, and through the regenerating influences of the Holy Spirit, might be enabled to bring forth the fruits of righteousness.

They rather conceive of Christianity as opening the door of mercy, that those who, on the ground of their own merits, could not have hoped to justify themselves before God, may yet be admitted, for Christ's sake, on condition of their having previously satisfied the moderated requisitions of divine justice. In speaking to others also of the Gospel plan, they are apt to talk too much of terms and performances on our part, on which we become entitled to an interest in the sufferings of Christ; instead of stating the benefits of Christ's satisfaction as extended to us freely, "without money and without price."

The practical consequences of these errors are such as might be expected. They tend to prevent that sense which we ought to entertain of our own natural misery and helplessness; and that deep feeling of gratitude for the sufferings, merits, and intercession of Christ, to which we are wholly indebted for our reconciliation to God, and for the will and the power, from first to last, to work out our own salvation.

They consider it too much in the light of a contract between two parties, wherein each, independently of the other, has his own distinct condition to perform; mankind —to do what they account their duty to be; God—to justify and accept them for Christ's sake. If they fail not in the discharge of their condition, assuredly the condition on God's part will be faithfully fulfilled.

Accordingly, we find, in fact, that those who represent the Gospel plan in the manner just described, give evidence of the subject with which their hearts are most filled by their proneness to run into merely moral disquisitions, either not

105

mentioning at all, or at least but cursorily touching on the sufferings and love of their Redeemer. They are little apt to kindle at their Savior's name, and, like the apostles, to be betrayed by their fervor into what may be almost an untimely descant on the riches of His unutterable mercy. In addressing others also whom they conceive to be living in habits of sin, and under the wrath of God, they rather advise them to amend their ways as a preparation for their coming to Christ, than to exhort them to throw themselves with deep prostration at the foot of the cross, there to obtain pardon and find grace to help in time of need. (See Hebrews 4:16.)

The great importance of the subject in question will justify having been thus particular. On a question of such magnitude, to mistake our meaning should be impossible. But after all which has been said, let it also be remembered, that except so far as the instruction of others is concerned, the point of importance is the internal disposition of the mind. The great question is where the dependence for pardon and for holiness is really placed, not what the language is in which people express themselves.

If this so generally prevailing error concerning the nature of the Gospel offer be in any considerable degree just, it will explain that so generally prevailing languor in the affections towards our blessed Savior which was formerly remarked, and that inadequate impression of the necessity and value of the assistance of the divine Spirit.

According to the soundest principles of reasoning, it may be also adduced as an additional proof of the correctness of our present statement, because they receive not that which is necessary to their nutriment and growth. If we would love Him as affectionately and rejoice in Him as triumphantly as the first Christians did, we must learn, like them, to repose our entire trust in Him, and to adopt the language of the apostle, "God forbid that I should glory, save in the cross of

our Lord Jesus Christ" (Galatians 6:14). "Who of God is
made unto us wisdom, and righteousness, and sanctification,
and redemption" (1 Corinthians 1: 30).

Doubtless there have been too many who, to their eternal
ruin, have abused the doctrine of salvation by grace and have
vainly trusted in Christ for pardon and acceptance, when by
their vicious lives they have plainly proved the groundlessness
of their pretensions. The tree is to be known by its fruits,
and there is too much reason to fear that there is no principle
of faith, when it does not decidedly evince itself by the fruits
of holiness.

Dreadful indeed will be the doom, above all others, of
those loose professors of Christianity, to whom at the last
day our blessed Savior will say these words, "I never knew
you; depart from me, ye that work iniquity." But the danger
of error on this side ought not to render us insensible to the
opposite error; an error against which in these days it seems
particularly necessary to guard.

For, even admitting that the persons above mentioned,
particularly the last class, do basically rely on the Atonement
of Christ; yet on their scheme, it must necessarily happen,
that the object to which they are most accustomed to look,
from which they most habitually derive complacency, is rather
their own qualified merit and services, though confessed to
be inadequate, than the sufferings and atoning death of a
crucified Savior.

But the danger of error on this side ought not to render
us insensible to the opposite error—an error against which
in these days it seems particularly necessary to guard. It is
far from my intention to enter into the niceties of controversy;
but surely I may be permitted to contend, that those who in
the main believe the doctrines of the Church of England, are
bound to allow that our dependence on our blessed Savior,
as alone the meritorious cause of our acceptance with God,

and as the means of all its blessed fruits and glorious consequences, must be not merely formal and nominal, but real and substantial—not vague, qualified, and partial, but direct, cordial, and entire. "Repentance towards God, and faith towards our Lord Jesus Christ," was the sum of the apostolic instructions. It is not an occasional invocation of the name or a transient recognition of the authority of Christ that fills up the measure of the term, "believing in Jesus."

This we shall find no such easy task; and if we trust that we do believe, we should all perhaps do well to cry out in the words of an imploring suppliant (he supplicated not in vain), "Lord, help thou our unbelief." We must be deeply conscious of our guilt and misery, heartily repenting of our sins, and firmly resolving to forsake them, and thus penitently "fleeing for refuge to the hope set before us." We must discover altogether on the merit of the crucified Redeemer our hopes of escape from the deserved punishment for our sins and of deliverance from their enslaving power. This must be our first, our last, our only plea. We are to surrender ourselves up to Him to "be washed in his blood" (Revelation 1:5), to be sanctified by His Spirit, resolving to receive Him as our Lord and Master, to learn in His school, and to obey all His commandments.

We would still more particularly address ourselves to others who are disposed to believe that, though, in some obscure and vague sense, the death of Christ, as the satisfaction for our sins, and for the purchase of our future happiness, and the sanctifying influence of the Holy Spirit, are to be admitted as fundamental articles of our creed, yet that these are doctrines so much above us, that they are not objects suited to our capacities; and that, turning our eyes from these difficult speculations, we should fix them on the practical and moral precepts of the Gospel.

"These," they allege, "it most concerns us to know; these, therefore, let us study. Such is the frailty of our nature, such the strength and number of our temptations to evil, that in reducing the Gospel morality to practice, we shall find full employment: and by attending to these moral precepts, rather than to those high mysterious doctrines which you are pressing on us, we shall best prepare to appear before God on that tremendous day, when 'He shall judge every man according to his works.'

To reply in the words of our blessed Savior, and of His beloved disciple: "This is the work of God, that ye believe on him whom he hath sent" (John 6:29). "This is his commandment, that we should believe on the name of his Son Jesus Christ" (1 John 3:23). In truth, if we consider but for a moment the opinions of men who argue that our acceptance by God is based on attending to moral principles, we must be conscious of their absurdity.

This may be not inconsistently the language of the modern Unitarian, but surely it is in the highest degree unreasonable to admit into our scheme all the grand peculiarities of Christianity, and having admitted, to neglect and think no more of them! "Wherefore," (might the Socinian say) "wherefore all this costly and complicated machinery? It is so little like the simplicity of nature, it is so unworthy of the divine hand, that it even offends against those rules of propriety which we require to be observed in the imperfect compositions of the human intellect."

Well may the Socinian assume this lofty tone with those whom we are now addressing. If these are indeed the doctrines of revelation, common sense suggests to us that from their nature and their magnitude they deserve our most serious regard. It is the very theology of Epicurus to allow the existence of these "heavenly things," but to deny their connection with human concerns, and their influence on human actions. Besides the unreasonableness of this conduct, we might strongly urge also in this connection the profaneness of thus treating as matters of subordinate consideration those parts of the system of Christianity which are so strongly impressed on our reverence by the dignity of the person to whom they relate. This very argument is indeed repeatedly and pointedly pressed by the sacred writers.

Nor is the profane irreverence of this conduct more striking than its ingratitude is. When, from reading that our Savior was "the brightness of his Father's glory, and the express image of his person, upholding all things by the word of his power," we go on to consider the purpose for which He came to earth, and all that He did and suffered for us; surely if we have a spark of ingenuousness left, we shall condemn ourselves as guilty of the blackest ingratitude, in rarely noticing, or coldly turning away, on whatever shallow pretences, from the contemplation of these miracles of mercy. For those minds, however, on which fear alone can operate, that motive is super-added: and we are plainly forewarned, both directly and indirectly, by the example of the Jewish nation, that God will not hold them guiltless who are thus unmindful of His most signal acts of condescension and kindness. But as this is a question of pure revelation, reasoning from probability may not be deemed decisive.

To revelation, therefore, we must appeal; and, as it might be to trespass on the reader's patience fully to discuss this most important subject, I must refer you to the sacred writings themselves for complete satisfaction. I would earnestly recommend it to you to weigh with the utmost seriousness those passages of Scripture wherein the peculiar doctrines of Christianity are expressly mentioned; and further, to attend with due regard to the illustration and confirmation which the conclusions resulting from those passages receive incidentally from the Word of God. Those who maintain the opinion which we are combating, will hereby become convinced that theirs is indeed an unscriptural religion; and will learn, instead of turning their eyes away from the grand peculiarities of Christianity, to keep these ever in view, as the first principles from which all the rest must derive their origin and receive their best support.[6]

Let us, then, solemnly ask ourselves whether we have fled for refuge to the appointed hope? And whether we are habitually looking to it, as to the only source of consolation? "Other foundation can no man lay:" There is no other ground of dependence, no other plea for pardon; but here there is hope, even to the uttermost.

Let us labor then to affect our hearts with a deep conviction of our need of a Redeemer, and of the value of His offered mediation. Let us fall down humbly before the throne of God, imploring pity and pardon in the name of the Son of' His love. Let us beseech Him to give us a true spirit of repentance and of hearty, undivided faith in the Lord Jesus. Let us not be satisfied till the cordiality of our belief be confirmed to us by that character of the apostle, "that to as many as believe Christ is precious" (1 Peter 2:7), and let us strive to increase daily in love towards our blessed Savior, and pray earnestly that "we may be filled with joy and peace in believing, that we may abound in hope, through the power of the Holy Ghost" (Romans 15:13).

Let us diligently put into practice the directions formerly given for cherishing and cultivating the principles of the love of Christ. With this view, let us labor assiduously to increase in knowledge, that ours may be a deeply rooted and rational affection. By frequent meditation on the incidents of our Savior's life, and still more on the astonishing circumstances of His death, by often calling to mind the state from which He proposes to rescue us, and the glories of His heavenly kingdom, by continual intercourse with Him through prayer and praise, of dependence and confidence in dangers, of hope and joy in our brighter hours, let us endeavor to keep Him constantly present in our minds, and to render all our conceptions of Him more distinct, lively, and intelligent. The title of Christian is a reproach to us if we estrange ourselves from Him, after whom we have been named.

The name of Jesus is not to be to us like the Allah of the Mohammedans, a talisman or an amulet to be worn on the arm, as an external badge merely, and a symbol of our profession, and to preserve us from evil by some mysterious and unintelligible potency, but it is to be engraved deeply on our hearts, there written by the finger of God himself in everlasting characters.

It is our title, known and understood to present peace and future glory. The assurance which it conveys of a bright reversion, will lighten the burdens and alleviate the sorrows of life; and in some happier moments it will impart to us a measure of that fullness of joy which is at God's right hand, enabling us to join even here in the heavenly hosanna, "Worthy is the Lamb that was slain, to receive power, and riches, and wisdom, and strength, and honor, and glory, and blessing." "Blessing, and honor, and glory, and power, be unto him that sitteth upon the throne, and unto the Lamb, for ever and ever" (Revelation 5:12-13).

FOOTNOTES

1 An adherent of a 16th-century Italian sect holding Unitarian views, including denial of the divinity of Jesus.
2 I see what is right, and approve it, but practice what is wrong.

3 The word "comfortless" is rendered in the margin, orphans.

4 See Dr. Doddridge's *Eight Sermons on Regeneration*, a most valuable compilation; and M'Laurin Essay on *Divine Grace*.

5 I trust that I will not be misunderstood to mean that any, continuing sinners and ungodly, can, by believing, be accepted or finally saved. Meanwhile, I will only remark that true faith (in which repentance is considered as necessarily involved) is in Scripture regarded as the radical principle of holiness. If the root exists, the proper fruits will be brought forth. An attention to this consideration would have easily explained and reconciled those passages of St. Paul's and St. James' epistles, which have furnished so much argument and criticism. St. James, it may be observed, all along speaks of a man, who does not have faith, but who says that he has faith. (James 2:14

Chapter Six

ON THE EXCELLENCE OF CHRISTIANITY

Having now completed a faint delineation of the leading features of real Christianity, we may point out some excellences which our faith really possesses, but which, as they are not to be found in that superficial system which so unworthily usurps its name, appear scarcely to have attracted sufficient notice, but by which our faith will appear to exhibit more clearly than, as Christianity is usually drawn, the characters of the divine original.

It holds true, indeed, in the case of Christianity, as in that of all the works of God, that though a superficial and cursory view cannot fail to help us discover something of their beauty; yet when, on a more careful and accurate scrutiny, we become better acquainted with their properties, we become also more deeply impressed by a conviction of their excellence. The intimate connection, that perfect harmony between the leading doctrines and the practical precepts of Christianity, which is apt to escape the attention of the ordinary eye, is one of the factors that makes Christianity so excellent.

It may not be improper to remark, though the position be so obvious as almost to render the statement of it needless, that there is the same close connection and perfect harmony in the leading doctrines of Christianity among each other. It is self-evident that the corruption of human nature, that our reconciliation to God by the Atonement of Christ, and that the restoration of our primitive dignity by the sanctifying influence of the Holy Spirit, are all parts of one whole, united in close dependence and mutual congruity.

Perhaps, however, it has not been sufficiently noticed, that in the chief practical precepts of Christianity, there is the same essential agreement, the same mutual dependency of one upon another. Let us survey this fresh instance of the wisdom of that system, which is the only solid foundation of our present or future happiness.

The virtues most strongly and repeatedly enjoined in Scripture, and by our progress in which we may best measure our advancement in holiness, are the fear and love of God and of Christ; love, kindness, and meekness towards our fellow-creatures; indifference to the possessions and events of this life, in comparison with our concern about eternal things; self-denial; and humility.

It has been already pointed out in many particulars, how essentially such of these Christian graces as respect the divine Being are connected with those which have more directly for their objects our fellow-creatures and ourselves. But in the case of these two last descriptions of Christian graces, the more attentively we consider them with reference to the acknowledged principles of human nature and to indisputable facts, the more we shall be convinced that they afford mutual aid towards the acquisition of each other; and that, when acquired, they all harmonize with each other in perfect and essential union.

This truth may perhaps be sufficiently apparent from what has been already stated, but it may not be useless to dwell on it a little more in detail. Take, then, the instances of loving-kindness and meekness towards others, and observe the solid foundation which is laid for them in self-denial, in moderation as to the good things of this life, and in humility.

The chief causes of enmity among people are pride and self-importance, the high opinion which people entertain of themselves, and the consequent deference which they exact from others; the over-valuation of worldly possessions and of worldly honors, and in consequence, a too eager competition for them. The rough edges of one man rub against those of another, if the expression may be allowed; and the friction is often such as to injure the works and disturb the just arrangements and regular motions of the social machine.

However, through Christianity all this roughness is filed down every wheel rolls smoothly in the performance of its appointed function, and there is nothing to retard the several movements, or break in upon the general order. The religious system indeed of the bulk of nominal Christians is satisfied with some appearances of virtue; and accordingly, while it recommends love and beneficence, it tolerates, as has been shown, pride and vanity in many cases; it even countenances and commends the excessive valuation of character, and at least allows a person's whole soul to be absorbed in the pursuit of the object he is following, be what it may, of personal or professional success.

But though these latter qualities may, for the most part, consist with a soft exterior and courtly demeanor, they cannot accord with the genuine internal principle of love. Some cause of discontent, some ground of jealousy or of envy will arise, some suspicion will corrode, some disappointment will sour, some slight or calumny will irritate, and provoke reprisals. In the higher walks of life, indeed, we learn to disguise our emotions; but such will be the real inward feelings of the soul, and they will frequently betray themselves when we are off our guard or when we are not likely to be disparaged by the discovery.

This state of the higher orders, in which people are scuffling eagerly for the same objects and wearing all the while such an appearance of sweetness and complacency, has often appeared to me to be not poorly illustrated by a gaming-table. There, every person is intent only on his or her own profit; the good success of one is the ill success of another, and therefore the general state of mind of the parties engaged at the gaming table may be pretty well conjectured.

All this, however, does not prevent, in well-bred societies, an exterior of perfect gentleness and good humor. But let the same employment be carried on among those who are not so well-schooled in the art of disguising their feelings; or in places where, by general connivance, people are allowed to give vent to their real emotions; and every passion will display itself, by which the "human face divine" can be distorted and deformed. The horrid name, by which it is familiarly known among its frequenters, sufficiently attests to the fidelity of its resemblance.

But Christianity requires the substantial reality, which may stand the scrutinizing eye of that Being "who searches the heart." This means, therefore, that the Christian should live and breathe in an atmosphere of benevolence. True Christianity forbids whatever can tend to obstruct its diffusion or vitiate its purity. It is on this principle that emulation is forbidden; for, besides that this passion almost insensibly degenerates into envy, and that it derives its origin chiefly from pride and a desire of self-exaltation, how can we easily love our neighbor as ourselves if we consider him or her at the same time as being our rival, and are intent upon surpassing him or her in the pursuit of whatever our competition might be?

Christianity, again, teaches us not to set our hearts on earthly possessions and earthly honors, and thereby provides for our really loving, or even cordially forgiving those who have been more successful than ourselves in the attainment of goals, or who have even designedly thwarted us in that pursuit. "Let the rich," says the apostle, "rejoice in that he is brought low."

How can he or she who means to attempt, in any degree to obey this precept be irreconcilably hostile towards anyone who may have been instrumental in his or her depression?

Christianity also teaches us not to prize human estimation at a very high level; and thereby provides for the practice of her injunction to love from the heart those who, justly or unjustly, may have attacked our reputation and wounded our character. She commands not the show, but the reality of meekness and gentleness; and by thus taking away the ailment of anger and the fomenters of discord, she provides for the maintenance of peace and the restoration of good temper among people, when they may have sustained a temporary interruption.

It is another capital excellence of Christianity that she values moral attainments at a far higher rate than intellectual acquisitions and proposes to conduct her followers to the height of virtue rather than of knowledge. On the contrary, most of the false religious systems which have prevailed in the world have proposed to reward the labor of their followers by drawing aside the veil which concealed from the vulgar eye their hidden mysteries and by introducing them to the knowledge of their deeper and more sacred doctrines.

This is eminently the case in the Hindu and Mohammedan religions, in the religions of China, and, for the most part, in the various modifications of ancient paganism. In systems which proceed on this principle, it is obvious that the bulk of mankind can never make any great proficiency. There was accordingly, among the nations of antiquity, one system, whatever it was, for the learned, and another for the illiterate.

Many of the philosophers spoke out, and professed to keep the lower orders in ignorance for the general good, plainly suggesting that the bulk of mankind was to be considered as almost of an inferior species. Aristotle himself countenanced this opinion. An opposite mode of proceeding naturally belongs to Christianity, which, without distinction, professes an equal regard for all human beings, and which was characterized by her first Promulgator as the Messenger of "glad tidings to the poor."

But Christianity's preference of moral to intellectual excellence is not to be praised only because it is congenial with its general character and suitable to the ends which our faith professes to have in view. It is the part of true wisdom to endeavor to excel, where we may really attain to excellence. This consideration might alone be sufficient to direct our efforts to the acquisition of virtue rather than of knowledge.

How limited is the range of the greatest human abilities! How scanty the stores of the richest human knowledge! Those who undeniably have held the first rank, both for natural and acquired endowments, instead of thinking their preeminence a just ground of self-exaltation, have commonly been the most forward to confess that their views were bounded and their attainments moderate. Had they indeed been less candid, this is a discovery which we would not have failed to make for ourselves. Experience daily furnishes us with examples of weakness and error, in the wisest and the most learned of individuals, which might serve to confound the pride of human wisdom.

Not so in morals. Made at first in the likeness of God, and still bearing about us some faint traces of our high original, we are offered by our blessed Redeemer the means of purification from our corruptions, and of once more regaining the image of our heavenly Father. (See Ephesians 2.) In love, the compendious expression for almost every virtue; in fortitude under all its forms; in justice, in humility, and in all the other graces of the Christian character, we are made capable of attaining to heights of real elevation. Were we but faithful in the use of the means of grace which we enjoy, the operations of the Holy Spirit, prompting and aiding our diligent endeavors, would infallibly crown our labors with success and make us partakers of a divine nature.

Let me not be thought to undervalue any of the gifts of God, or of the fruits of human exertion, but let not these be prized beyond their proper worth. If one of those little industrious ants, to which we have been well sent for a lesson of diligence and foresight, were to pride itself upon its strength, because it could carry off a larger grain of wheat than any other of its fellow-ants, should we not laugh at the vanity which could be highly gratified with such a contemptible preeminence? And is it far different to the eye of reason, when humans, weak, short-sighted humans, are vain of surpassing others in knowledge, in which, at best, their progress must be so limited; forgetting the true dignity of their nature, and the path which would conduct them to real excellence?

The unparalleled value of the precepts of Christianity ought not to be passed over altogether unnoticed in this place. It is by no means, however, the design of this little work to attempt to trace all the various excellences of Christianity; but it may not have been improper to point out a few particulars which have fallen under our notice, and hitherto perhaps may scarcely have been enough regarded. Every such instance, it should always be remembered, is a fresh proof of Christianity being a revelation from God.

It is still less, however, my intention to attempt to vindicate the divine origin of our holy religion. This task has often been executed by far abler advocates than me. Eager, however, in my little measure, to contribute to the support of this great cause, may it be permitted me to state one argument which impresses my mind with particular force. This is the great variety of the kinds of evidence which have been adduced in proof of Christianity, and the confirmation thereby afforded of its truth: the proof from prophecy—from miracles—from the character of Christ—from that of His apostles—from the nature of the doctrines of Christianity—from the nature and excellence of her practical precepts—from the accordance we have lately pointed out between the doctrinal and practical system of Christianity, whether considered each in itself or in their mutual relation to each other—from other species of internal evidence, afforded in the more abundance in proportion as the sacred records have been scrutinized with greater care—from the accounts of contemporary or nearly contemporary writers—from the impossibility of accounting, on any other supposition than that of the truth of Christianity, for its promulgation and early prevalence. These and other lines of argument have all been brought forward and ably urged by different writers, in proportion as they have struck the minds of different observers more or less forcibly

Now, granting that some obscure and illiterate men, residing in a distant province of the Roman Empire, had plotted to impose a forgery upon the world; though some foundation for the imposture might, and indeed must have been attempted to be laid; it seems, at least to my understanding, morally impossible that so many different species of proofs, and all so strong, should have lent their concurrent aid, and have united their joint force in the establishment of the falsehood.

It may assist the reader in estimating the value of this argument, to consider upon how different a footing, in this respect, has rested every other religious system, without exception, which was ever proposed to the world; and, indeed, every other historical fact, of which the truth has been at all contested.

Dear reader, it is impossible to overestimate the excellence of true Christianity—the Christianity of our Lord Jesus Christ.

Part 3

TRIBUTES TO

William Wilberforce

EPISTLE TO WILLIAM WILBERFORCE, ESQ. ON THE REJECTION OF THE BILL FOR ABOLISHING THE SLAVE TRADE

by Anna Lætitia Barbauld (1743-1825)

Cease, Wilberforce, to urge thy generous aim!
Thy Country knows the sin, and stands the shame!
The Preacher, Poet, Senator in vain
Has rattled in her sight the Negro's chain;

With his deep groans assail'd her startled ear,
And rent the veil that hid his constant tear;
Forc'd her averted eyes his stripes to scan,
Beneath the bloody scourge laid bare the man,
Claimed Pity's tear, urged Conscience' strong controul,
And flash'd conviction on her shrinking soul.
The Muse, too soon awaked, with ready tongue
At Mercy's shrine applausive peals rung;
And Freedom's eager sons, in vain foretold
A new Astrean reign, an age of gold:
She knows and she persists–Still Afric bleeds,
Uncheck'd, the human traffic still proceeds;
She stamps her infamy to future time,
And on her harden'd forehead seals the crime.

In vain, to thy white standard gathering round,
Wit, Worth, and Parts and Eloquence are found:
In vain, to push to birth thy great design,
Contending chiefs, and hostile virtues join;
All, from conflicting ranks, of power possest
To rouse, to melt, or to inform the breast.
Where seasoned tools of Avarice prevail,
A Nation's eloquence, combined, must fail:
Each flimsy sophistry by turns they try;
The plausive argument, the daring lye,
The artful gloss, that moral sense confounds,
Th' acknowledged thirst of gain that honour wounds:
Bane of ingenuous minds, th' unfeeling sneer,
Which, sudden, turns to stone the falling tear:
They search assiduous, with inverted skill,
For forms of wrong, and precedents of ill;
With impious mockery wrest the sacred page,
And glean up crimes from each remoter age:
Wrung Nature's tortures, shuddering, while you tell,
From scoffing fiends bursts forth the laugh of hell;

In Britain's senate, Misery's pangs give birth
To jests unseemly, and to horrid mirth–
Forbear!–thy virtues but provoke our doom,
And swell th' account of vengeance yet to come;
For, not unmarked in Heaven's impartial plan,
Shall man, proud worm, contemn his fellowman?
And injur'd Afric, by herself redrest,
Darts her own serpents at her Tyrant's breast.

Each vice, to minds deprav'd by bondage known,
With sure contagion fastens on his own;
In sickly languors melts his nerveless frame,
And blows to rage impetuous Passion's flame:

Fermenting swift, the fiery venom gains
The milky innocence of infant veins;
There swells the stubborn will, damps learning's fire,
The whirlwind wakes of uncontroul'd desire,
Sears the young heart to images of woe,
And blasts the buds of Virtue as they blow.

Lo! where reclin'd, pale Beauty courts the breeze,
Diffus'd on sofas of voluptuous ease;
With anxious awe, her menial train around,
Catch her faint whispers of half-utter'd sound;

See her, in monstrous fellowship, unite
At once the Scythian, and the Sybarite;
Blending repugnant vices, misally'd,
Which *frugal* nature purpos'd to divide;
See her, with indolence to fierceness join'd,
Of body delicate, infirm of mind,
With languid tones imperious mandates urge;
With arm recumbent wield the household scourge;
And with unruffled mien, and placid sounds,
Contriving torture, and inflicting wounds.

Nor, in their palmy walks and spicy groves,
The form benign of rural Pleasure roves;
No milk-maid's song, or hum of village talk,
Soothes the lone poet in his evening walk:
No willing arm the flail unweary'd plies,
Where the mix'd sounds of cheerful labour rise;
No blooming maids, and frolic swains are seen
To pay gay homage to their harvest queen:
No heart-expanding scenes their eyes must prove
Of thriving industry, and faithful love:
But shrieks and yells disturb the balmy air,

Dumb sullen looks of woe announce despair,
And angry eyes thro' dusky features glare.
Far from the sounding lash the Muses fly,
And sensual riot drowns each finer joy.

Nor less from the gay East, on essenc'd wings,
Breathing unnam'd perfumes, Contagion springs;

The soft luxurious plague alike pervades
The marble palaces, and rural shades;
Hence throng'd Augusta builds her rosy bowers,
And decks in summer wreaths her smoky towers;
And hence, in summer bow'rs, Art's costly hand
Pours courtly splendours o'er the dazzled land:
The manners melt–One undistinguish'd blaze
O'erwhelms the sober pomp of elder days;
Corruption follows with gigantic stride,
And scarce vouchsafes his shameless front to hide:
The spreading leprosy taints ev'ry part,
Infects each limb, and sickens at the heart.
Simplicity! most dear of rural maids,
Weeping resigns her violated shades:

Stern Independence from his globe retires,
And anxious Freedom eyes her drooping fires;
By foreign wealth are British morals chang'd,
And Afric's sons, and India's, smile aveng'd.

For you, whose temper'd ardour long has borne
Untir'd the labour, and unmov'd the scorn;
In Virtue's fast be inscrib'd your fame,
And utter'd your's with Howard's honour'd name,
Friends of the friendless–Hail, ye generous band!
Whose efforts yet arrest Heav'n's lifted hand,

Around whose steady brows, in union bright,
The civic wreath, and Christian's palm unite:

Your merit stands, no greater and no less,
Without, or with the varnish of success;
But seek no more to break a Nation's fall,
For ye have sav'd yourselves–and that is all.
Succeeding times your struggles, and their fate,
With mingled shame and triumph shall relate,
While faithful History, in her various page,
Marking the features of this motley age,
To shed a glory, and to fix a stain,
Tells how you strove, and that you strove in vain.

First Publication: *Epistle to William Wilberforce, Esq. on the Rejection of the Bill for Abolishing the Slave Trade*, by Anna Lætitia Barbauld. London: Printed for J. Johnson, No. 72, St. Paul's Church-Yard, 1791.

Chapter Eight

NEWSPAPER ACCOUNTS OF
WILBERFORCE'S FUNERAL

*Following William Wilberforce's death, major newspapers
around the world carried the story. Here are two that
typify how the news was reported in those days.*

NEW YORK DAILY ADVOCATE

The death of Mr. Wilberforce brings back the mind
irresistibly to the memorable events of his history, and forces
upon the recollection the extraordinary virtues which adorned
and ennobled his character, and placed him at the head of
the long catalogue of philanthropists of the last half century.

In the early part of his life and soon after, he took a seat
in the House of Commons, where he commenced a
parliamentary warfare against the slave trade. Aided by some
of the ablest statesmen in the kingdom, and assisted by a
number of benevolent individuals, whose principles and
feelings fully corresponded with his own, in spite of every
obstruction, in the face of defeat after defeat, and in utter
disregard of obloquy and reproach, he persevered for twenty
years in his most honorable and praiseworthy career, until
his efforts were crowned with success. In the year 1807, if
we recollect right, Parliament passed a law prohibiting that

diabolical traffic, and ridding the nation so far of that most iniquitous and disgraceful system.

By one of those untoward circumstances which occur in the history of nations, when the Constitution of the United States was formed and adopted, a provision was suffered lo be incorporated in it, denying to Congress the power of prohibiting the slave trade before 1808. In 1807, and by an almost contemporaneous net, Congress passed a law declaring that the slave trade should cease after the time prescribed in the constitution.

Having witnessed the eventual success of his long continued and most meritorious efforts in the case of justice and humanity, but considering his work as only half-done, he commenced a series of measures intended to complete the great work, thus fortunately in part accomplished. This was the abolition of slavery throughout the British colonial dominions. To bring about this great result, unexampled efforts were made to enlist public opinion in its favor—associations were formed, unceasing exertions were employed to collect information, and diffuse it throughout the kingdom, and the presses to a considerable extent engaged in the enterprise; and a single periodical publication the *Christian Observer*, pursued the object with the utmost assiduity, by the exercise of great talents, and the most unshaken independence.

Every year, when the subject was brought before Parliament, showed a strong accession of strength in favor of the cause; when in 1821, if we have the date correctly, Mr. Canning's resolutions, in favor of effectual abolition, were carried through Parliament. Having now a firm foot-hold on which to rest, the great Object was pursued with renewed zeal and vigor, all the weight and force of national opinion was brought to bear upon the question, which was altogether irresistible. When it became apparent that abolition could be no longer resisted, opposition was to a great degree given up, and the only question of any moment that remained to be discussed was that of compensation. During the present session of Parliament, a resolution in favor of emancipation has passed both houses, and nothing now remains to carry the measure into effect, but to decide upon the details of the bill, and this black stain upon the character of the British nation and government will be effaced.

Mr. Wilberforce's life was providentially continued until this great measure was so far consummated, when his earthly career was brought to a close, and he was called, as there are the strongest reasons for believing, to the happiness and the glory of a better world.

History scarcely furnishes any account of an uninspired man of greater moral worth, more active philanthropy, more extensive usefulness, than Mr. Wilberforce. His life was devoted to the service of God, and the good of his fellow men. His piety was as sincere and ardent as his benevolence, and both were uniformly conspicuous throughout a long and useful life. His life is now closed, but he has left behind him a character of the highest elevation for purity of principle and moral rectitude, and at the same time, equally distinguished for practical utility and benevolence to the human race.

A London newspaper account:

FUNERAL OF THE LATE MR. WILBERFORCE

The funeral of that most excellent man, Mr. Wilberforce, eminent through the course of his long life for his public and private virtues, for his sterling patriotism, his Christian piety, and his universal feeling of philanthropy, took place on Saturday. It was at first intended, in conformity to the wish of the deceased, to conduct his funeral with the utmost privacy, and to inter his remains in Newington church yard; but a very considerable number of the most distinguished Members of the Houses of Peers and Commons, anxious to pay a last tribute of respect to the memory of a man, who through a long series of years, had been so honorably distinguished in the British Senate, prevailed on his sons and immediate friends to allow the funeral to be a public one, and the place of interment to be Westminster Abbey, that solemn habitation of " the departed great;" thus conferring the highest possible honor on the memory of Mr. Wilberforce, and giving to the world (for of Mr. Wilberforce it may be said, that he was not the properly of a nook, but of the world) an exalted testimony of the country, and of friendship which his mild manners and noble qualities had won him.

At about half past twelve o'clock, the Order of the Procession having been arranged, the coffin, containing the remains of the deceased, was placed in the hearse, and the procession began to move in the following order:

Horsemen, two and two abreast, wearing black scarves and hat bands, and preceded by Mr. Birch, the family undertaker.
Two Mules abreast.
Plume of Feathers.
Two Mules abreast.
Attends.
Horsemen, two and two abreast.
Attends.
Hearse (bearing the coffin,
Richly studded with black plumes, and
Drawn by six jet Horses, richly
Caparisoned, with black velvet trappings,
And adorned with nodding plumes.

Eight Mourning Coaches.
The first bearing the Deceased's Sons,
As Chief Mourners,
The others containing the Mourners.
Noblemen and Gentlemen's Carriages,
To the number of nearly Fifty,
being chiefly those of the Members of both Houses of
Parliament.

In this manner the Procession moved slowly from
Cadogan Place towards Westminster Abbey, forming a very
lengthened train, accompanied by immense crowds of people,
who flanked it in moving columns, on either side; and at a
little after one o'clock, the signal that it was approaching the
Abbey was given) by Mr. Lee, the High Constable of
Westminster, to the Peers and Commoners, who had
assembled in their relative Houses of Parliament for the
purpose of following the body in procession through the isles
of the Abbey.

The Peers, amounting to a considerable number, all
dressed in deep black, having put on scarves and hat bands,
proceeded from the Jerusalem Chamber of the House of Lords
into the Abbey entering at Poet's Corner; while the Members
of the House of Commons, numbering between one and two
hundred, in full mourning, proceeded two abreast to the west
door of the Abbey, by which they entered.

The coffin, at this period, having arrived at the western
door, was moved from the hearse and placed on the shoulders
of six men, the pall of rich black velvet, with a deep boarder
of white satin, having been thrown over it. When inside the
door the bearers were ordered to halt; it was here a proud
sight to see the Royalty, the high station, rank and greatest
talent of the country, become the pall bearers of a virtuous
citizen, which was at once a compliment to the memory of

the man, a credit to their own hearts and understandings, and an honor of which the people of this great country may proudly boast to other nations.

The following are the names of the distinguished individuals who supported the pull:

The Lord Chancellor, Speaker of the House of Commons, Lord Bexley, and the Marquess of Westminster on the one side; the Right Honourable Charles Grant, Sir Robert Ingis, Mr. W. Smith (as we are informed), and his Royal Highness the Duke of Gloucester on the other; His Royal Highness was the last on the extreme right—it being a rule according to the etiquette of such occasions for Royalty to be last amongst the pall bearers—the Lord Chancellor was first on the extreme left.

A solemn stillness now prevailed, amidst which the order of the procession through the aisles was formed, and the fight was altogether a most impressive one. The King's Boys in their uniforms, and the Westminster School Boys, in their white surplices, two and two abreast, formed the van of the procession. The Abbey Choristers, robed in their robes of white and scarlet, together with the Choristers of St. Paul's Cathedral, Whitehall Chapel, and the various other important places of public worship throughout the metropolis next followed; then followed the Peers, at the head of whom was his Royal Highness the Duke of Sussex and his Grace the Duke of Wellington, both in deep black, and exhibiting a star on the left breast: next in order were the Archbishop of Canterbury, the Bishop of Chichester, and various other Bishops; after them followed the Dean and Chapter of Westminster, then the Rev. Dr. Holcombo, accompanied by the Rev. Dr. Deukins, next to them the coffin and distinguished pallbearers, and lastly, the Members of the House of Commons, two and two abreast. During all this time the Abbey bell; tolled slowly and solemnly, and the procession having been arranged, the signal to advance was given.

The organ here commenced its melancholy and devotional funeral notes, the choristers chiming in with a sweetness and solemnity of voice, producing, as the sounds travelled from aisle to aisle, the deepest feeling that the presence of man's mortality and immortality can inspire. The Choristers, as the procession moved towards the north transept of the Abbey, where the grave was formed, close to the tombs of Canning, Fox, and Pitt, chanted the funeral dirge composed by Croft. Having arrived at the grave, the coffin was lowered into it, and the funeral service was most impressively read by the Rev. Dr. Holcombe, the Choristers and King's Boys, &c. chanting in occasionally with the accompaniment of the organ. During this most solemn part of the service, their Royal Highnesses the Dukes of Sussex and Gloucester, the Duke of Wellington, the Archbishop of Canterbury, the Bishop of Chichester, and the various other Bishops, the Lord Chancellor, the Speaker of the House of Commons, and the other Pall Bearers, the Marquess of Lansdown, Lord Roslyn, Lord Althorp, Lord Auckland, &c. formed a circle around the grave.

Amongst the distinguished Commoners present, besides those already mentioned, we observed Sir James Graham, Sir Robert Peel, Lord Murpeth, Mr. Fowel Buxton, Dr. Lushington, Mr. Stanley, Mr. Lyttlelon, Sir Robert Grant, Mr. Spring Rice, the Messrs. Attwood, Messrs. James and Henry Grattan, Mr. Tynte, Mr. Carew O'Dwyer, &c.

Besides the above, the Abbey was crowded by persons of distinction, amongst whom were many ladies.

After the funeral service was over, the numerous persons present pressed eagerly towards the grave to get a sight of the coffin, which was covered with rich black velvet and ornamented with gilt moulding, heading, etc. In the centre of the lid was a splendid brass plate, of considerable dimensions, with the following simple inscription:

WILLIAM WILBERFORCE, Esq.
Born 24th of August, 1759
Died 29th of July, 1833

Thus terminated the mortal career of as pure and virtuous a public man as ever lived—of "a man whom (in the words of Ben Johnson) no sordid hope of gain, or frosty apprehension of danger, could make a parasite to time, or place, or opinion."

Mr. Wilberforce's public life forms one of the brightest pages in the annals of this country, so long renowned amongst the nations of the earth. By his exertions in the Senate, the heart of the nation was first impressed with the horror and degradation of its long cherished traffic in human beings. His glowing eloquence inspired in others the feelings of humanity in which it had its source, and he had the glory of witnessing the triumph of that holy cause to which he had devoted all the energies of his gifted mind, in the deliverance of his country from the abomination of the Slave Trade—a consummation well characterized by one of his ablest coadjutors as "the saving of the soul of the nation." A delicate constitution compelled him to retire from Parliament and public life some years ago, which deprived the cause of humanity of his personal exertions in the total extinction of slavery; but the feelings he mainly contributed to inspire can never die; and the people of this country, while they honor the name of Wilberforce, will feel their own highest honor in imitating the conduct of him whose benevolence, founded on the sincerest piety, regarded the whole human race as friends and brothers.

The funeral ceremony did not terminate before three o'clock. We may here mention that we saw two gentlemen of color in the procession, which appeared to feel a deep interest in the solemnity of the passing scene.

Chapter Nine

WILLIAM COWPER'S POEMS

The Negro's Complaint
by William Cowper

FORCED from home and all its pleasures
Afric's coast I left forlorn,
To increase a stranger's treasures
O'er the raging billows borne.
Men from England bought and sold me,
Paid my price in paltry gold;
But, though slave they have enrolled me,
Minds are never to be sold.

Still in thought as free as ever,
What are England's rights, I ask,
Me from my delights to sever,
Me to torture, me to task?
Fleecy locks and black complexion
Cannot forfeit nature's claim;
Skins may differ, but affection
Dwells in white and black the same.

Why did all-creating nature
Make the plant for which we toil?

Sighs must fan it, tears must water,
Sweat of ours must dress the soil.
Think, ye masters iron-hearted,
Lolling at your jovial boards,
Think how many backs have smarted
For the sweets your cane affords.
Is there, as ye sometimes tell us,

Is there One who reigns on high?
Has He bid you buy and sell us,
Speaking from his throne, the sky?
Ask Him, if your knotted scourges,
Matches, blood-extorting screws,
Are the means that duty urges
Agents of His will to use?

Hark! He answers!—Wild tornadoes
Strewing yonder sea with wrecks,
Wasting towns, plantations, meadows,
Are the voice with which He speaks.
He, foreseeing what vexations
Afric's sons should undergo,
Fixed their tyrants' habitations
Where His whirlwinds answer—"No."

By our blood in Africa wasted
Ere our necks received the chain;
By the miseries that we tasted,
Crossing in your barks the main;
By our sufferings, since ye brought us
To the man-degrading mart,
All sustained by patience, taught us
Only by a broken heart;

Deem our nation brutes no longer,
Till some reason ye shall find
Worthier of regard and stronger
Than the colour of our kind.
Slaves of gold, whose sordid dealings
Tarnish all your boasted powers,
Prove that you have human feelings,
Ere you proudly question ours!

PITY FOR POOR AFRICANS (1788)
By William Cowper

I OWN I am shock'd at the purchase of slaves,
And fear those who buy them and sell them are knaves;
What I hear of their hardships, their tortures, and groans
Is almost enough to draw pity from stones.

I pity them greatly, but I must be mum,
For how could we do without sugar and rum?
Especially sugar, so needful we see?
What? Give up our desserts, our coffee, and tea!

Besides, if we do, the French, Dutch, and Danes,
Will heartily thank us, no doubt, for our pains;
If we do not buy the poor creatures, they will,
And tortures and groans will be multiplied still.

If foreigners likewise would give up the trade,
Much more in behalf of your wish might be said;
But while they get riches by purchasing blacks,
Pray tell me why we may not also go snacks?
Your scruples and arguments bring to my mind
A story so pat, you may think it is coin'd,

On purpose to answer you, out of my mint;
But, I can assure you, I saw it in print.
A youngster at school, more sedate than the rest,
Had once his integrity put to the test;
His comrades had plotted an orchard to rob,
And ask'd him to go and assist in the job.

He was shock'd, sir, like you, and answer'd—"Oh, no
What! Rob our good neighbour! pray you, don't go;
Besides, the man's poor, his orchard's his bread,
Then think of his children, for they must be fed."

"You speak very fine, and you look very grave,
But apples we want, and apples we'll have;
If you will go with us, you shall have a share,
If not, you shall have neither apple nor pear."

They spoke, and Tom ponder'd—I see they will go:
Poor man! What a pity to injure him so.
Poor man! I would save him his fruit if I could,
But staying behind will do him no good.

"If the matter depended alone upon me,
His apples might hang till they dropt from the tree;
But, since they will take them, I think I'll go too,
He will lose none by me, though I get a few."

His scruples thus silenc'd, Tom felt more at ease,
And went with his comrades the apples to seize;
He blam'd and protested, but join'd in the plan;
He shar'd in the plunder, but pitied the man.

Chapter Ten

SPIRIT OF THE AGE
A Contemporary Evaluates Wilberforce

Mr. Wilberforce is a less perfect character in his way. He acts from mixed motives. He would willingly serve two masters, God and Mammon. He is a person of many excellent and admirable qualifications, but he has made a mistake in wishing to reconcile those that are incompatible. He has a most winning eloquence, specious, persuasive, familiar, silver-tongued, is amiable, charitable, conscientious, pious, loyal, humane, tractable to power, accessible to popularity, honouring the king, and no less charmed with the homage of his fellow-citizens. "What lacks he then?" Nothing but an economy of good parts. By aiming at too much, he has spoiled all, and neutralized what might have been an estimable character, distinguished by signal services to mankind. A man must take his choice not only between virtue and vice, but between different virtues. Otherwise, he will not gain his own approbation, or secure the respect of others. The graces and accomplishments of private life mar the man of business and the statesman. There is a severity, sternness, a self-denial, and a painful sense of duty required in the one, which ill-befits the softness and sweetness which should characterise the other. Loyalty, patriotism, friendship, humanity, are all virtues; but may they not sometimes clash?

By being unwilling to forego the praise due to any, we may forfeit the reputation of all; and, instead of uniting the suffrages of the whole world in our favour, we may end in becoming a sort of by-word for affectation, cant, hollow professions, trimming, fickleness, and effeminate imbecility. It is best to choose and act up to some one leading character, as it is best to have some settled profession or regular pursuit in life.

We can readily believe that Mr. Wilberforce's first object and principle of action is to do what he thinks right: his next (and that we fear is of almost equal weight with the first) is to do what will be thought so by other people. He is always at a game of hawk and buzzard between these two: his "conscience will not budge," unless the world goes with it. He does not seem greatly to dread the denunciation in Scripture, but rather to court it—"Woe unto you, when all men shall speak well of you!" We suspect he is not quite easy in his mind, because West-India planters and Guinea traders do not join in his praise. His ears are not strongly enough tuned to drink in the execrations of the spoiler and the oppressor as the sweetest music. It is not enough that one half of the human species (the images of God carved in ebony, as old Fuller calls them) shout his name as a champion and a saviour through vast burning zones, and moisten their parched lips with the gush of gratitude for deliverance from chains—he must have a Prime-Minister drink his health at a Cabinet dinner for aiding to rivet on those of his country and of Europe! He goes hand and heart along with Government in all their notions of legitimacy and political aggrandizement, in the hope that they will leave him a sort of no-man's ground of humanity in the Great Desert, where his reputation for benevolence and public spirit may spring up and flourish, till its head touches the clouds, and it stretches out its branches to the furthest part of the earth. He has no mercy on those who claim a property in Negro slaves as so much livestock on their estates; the country rings with the applause of his wit, his eloquence, and his indignant appeals to common sense and humanity on this subject—but not a word has he to say, not a whisper does he breathe against the claim set up by the Despots of the Earth over their Continental subjects, but does every thing in his power to confirm and sanction it! He must give no offence. Mr. Wilberforce's humanity will go all lengths that it can with safety and discretion: but it is not to be supposed that it should lose him his seat for Yorkshire, the smiles of Majesty, or the countenance of the loyal and pious. He is anxious to do all the good he can without hurting himself or his fair fame. His conscience and his character compound matters very amicably. He rather patronizes honesty than is a martyr to it. His patriotism, his philanthropy are not so ill-bred, as to quarrel with his loyalty or to banish him from the first circles. He preaches vital Christianity to untutored savages; and tolerates its worst abuses in civilized states. He thus shows his part for religion without offending the clergy, or circumscribing its sphere of his usefulness. There is in all this an appearance of a good deal of cant and tricking. His patriotism may be accused ill being servile; his humanity ostentatious: his loyalty conditional; his religion a mixture of fashion and fanaticism. "Out upon such half-faced fellowship!" Mr. Wilberforce has the pride of being familiar with the great; the vanity of being popular; the conceit of an approving conscience. He is coy in his approaches to power: his public spirit is, in a mariner, under the rose. He thus reaps the credit of independence, without the obloquy; and secures the advantages of servility, without incurring any obligations. He has two strings to his tow: he by no means neglects his worldly interests, while he expects a bright reversion in the skies. Mr. Wilberforce is far from being a hypocrite; but he is, we think, as fine a specimen of moral equivocation as can well be conceived. A hypocrite is one who is the very reverse of, or who despises the character he pretends to be: Mr. Wilberforce would be all that he pretends to be, and he is it in fact, as far as words, plausible theories, good inclinations, and easy services go, but not in heart and soul, or so as to give up the appearance of any one of his pretensions to preserve the reality of any other. He carefully chooses his ground to fight the battles of loyalty, religion, and humanity, and it is such us is always safe and advantageous to himself! This is perhaps hardly fair, and it is of dangerous or doubtful tendency. Lord Eldon, for instance, is known to be a thorough-paced ministerialist: his opinion is only that of his party. But Mr. Wilberforce is not a party-man. He is the more looked up to on this account, but not with sufficient reason. By tampering with different temptations and personal projects, he has all the air of the most perfect independence, and gains a character for impartiality and candour, when he is only striking a balance in his mind between the éclat of differing from a Minister on some vantage ground, and the risk or odium that may attend it. He carries all the weight of his artificial popularity over to the. Government on vital points and hard-run questions; while they, in return, lend him a little of the gilding of court-favour to set off his disinterested philanthropy and tramontane enthusiasm. As a leader or a follower, he makes an odd jumble of interests. By virtue of religious sympathy, he has brought the Saints over to the side of the abolition of Negro slavery. This his adversaries think hard and stealing a march upon them. What have the SAINTS to do with freedom or reform of any kind? Mr. Wilberforce's style of speaking is not quite parliamentary; it is halfway between that and evangelical. He is altogether a double-entendre: the very tone of his voice is a double-entendre. It winds, and undulates, and glides up and down on texts of Scriptures, and scraps from Paley, and trite sophistry, and pathetic appeals to his hearers in a faltering, inprogressive, sidelong way, like those birds of weak wing that are borne from their straightforward course: "By every little breath that under heaven is blown."

Something of this fluctuating, time-serving principle was visible even in the great question of the Abolition of the Slave Trade. He was, at one time, half inclined to surrender it into Mr. Pitt's dilatory hands, and seemed to think the gloss of novelty was gone from it, and the gaudy colouring of popularity sunk into the sable ground from which it rose! It was, however, persisted in and carried to a triumphant conclusion. Mr. Wilberforce said too little on this occasion of one, compared with whom he was but the frontispiece to that great chapter in the history of the world—the mask, the varnishing, and painting—the man that effected it by Herculean labours of body, and equally gigantic labours of mind was Clarkson, the true Apostle of human Redemption on that occasion, and who, it is remarkable, resembles in his person and lineaments more than one of the Apostles in the Cartoons of Raphael. He deserves to be added to the Twelve!

The Spirit of the Age: of Contemporary Portraits
Author Unknown
Publisher: Wiley & Putnam, New York, NY
Published in 1846

Chapter Eleven

TRIBUTE TO WILLIAM WILBERFORCE

By William Jay

MY DEAR SIR—I am not certain that my motive was quite pure, when I felt a very powerful desire that, in a way of some little publicity and continuance, I might appear associated with one so esteemed and illustrious as the man whose name dignifies this page, and at whose feet I presume to lay this volume.

A writer of judgment and wit has somewhere said, that "there are good persons with whom it will be soon enough to be acquainted in heaven." But there are individuals with whom it is no common privilege to have been acquainted on earth.

It is now more than forty years since the writer of this address was indulged and honored with your notice and friendship. During this period—so long in the brevity of human life!—he has had many opportunities of deriving great pleasure and profit from your private conversation; and also of observing, in your public career, the proofs you displayed of the orator, the statesman, the advocate of enlightened freedom, and the feeling, fearless, persevering, and successful opponent of a traffic that is "a reproach to any people." But he would be unworthy of the ministry he fills, and be ashamed of the age he has now reached, as a professed follower of our Lord and Saviour, if he could not increasingly say, with Young, "A CHRISTIAN is the highest style of man."

All other greatness is, in the view of faith, seducing and dangerous; in actual enjoyment unsatisfactory and vain, and in duration fleeting and momentary. "The world passeth away, and the lusts thereof: but he that doeth the will of God abideth for ever." [1 John 2:17] The expectation of the man who has his "portion in this life" is continually deteriorating: for every hour brings him nearer the loss of all his treasure; and "as he came forth of his mother's womb, naked shall he return to go as he came, and shall take nothing of his labor which he may carry away in his hand." But the "good hope through grace" [2 Thessalonians 2:16] which animates the believer, is always approaching its realities; and therefore grows, with the lapse of time, more valuable and more lively. As it is spiritual in its quality, and heavenly in its object, it does not depend on outward things, and is not affected with the decays of nature. Like the Glastonbury thorn, fabulously planted by Joseph of Arimathea, it blooms   in the depth of winter. It "brings forth fruit in old age." "At eventide it is light." "For which cause we faint not; but though our outward man perish, yet the inward man is renewed day by day." [2 Corinthians 4:16]

And this, my dear sir, you are now happily experiencing, at the close of more than "threescore years and ten." And I hail you, not as descending towards the grave under the applause of nations, but as an heir of immortality, "looking for the mercy of our Lord Jesus Christ unto eternal life." [Jude 21] Attended with the thanksgivings of the truly wise and good on your behalf, and in the comforts of the Holy Ghost, and with an unsullied religious reputation, you are finishing a course which you have been enabled to pursue through evil report and through good report; undeviatingly, unabatingly; forgetful of none of the claims of personal or relative godliness, amidst all the cares and engagements of a popularity peculiarly varied and extensive; neglecting, in addition to the influence of example, no means to recommend the one thing needful to others; and, even from the press, defending the interests of practical Christianity, in a work so widely circulated, go justly admired, and so preeminently useful, especially among the higher classes in society.

Nor can I omit the opportunity of acknowledging, individually, the obligations I feel myself under to your zeal and wisdom, when, in the novitiate of my ministry, your correspondence furnished me with hints of admonition, instruction, and encouragement, to which I owe much of any degree of acceptance and usefulness with which I have been favored. Nor can I forbear also to mention another benefactor, whose name I know is as dear to every feeling of your heart as it is to every feeling of my own—the Rev. John Newton. With this incomparable man I was brought into an early intimacy, in consequence of his addressing me without solicitation, and when personally unknown to him, in counsels and advice the most seasonable, just as I had emerged into public life, peculiarly young and inexperienced and exposed. These opportune advantages, for which I would be daily thankful, recall the exclamation of Solomon, "A word fitly spoken, how good is it!" [Proverbs 25:11] and lead me to lament that persons so seldom in this way seek or even seize opportunities of usefulness. How often do they omit to avail themselves of the influence which God, by their rank, or wisdom, or piety, or age, had given them over others for their good; though it is a talent for which they are responsible, and the use of which would often be as welcome in the exertion as important in the results.

The years which have passed over our acquaintance have been no ordinary ones. They have been signalized by some of the most important events that could affect other nations or our own. I am sufficiently aware of your sentiments, and fully accord with them in thinking that while, as men and citizens we cannot be indifferent to the state of public affairs, but ought to be alive to the welfare of a country that has such unexampled claims to our attachment and gratitude; yet that as Christians we should judge things by a rule of our own, and esteem those the best days in which the best cause nourishes most. Now while we have suffered much, and have had much to deplore, yet "the walls of the temple" have been rising "in troublous times," and our political gloom has been relieved by more than gleams of religious glory. Let us not ask with some, "What is the cause that the former days were better than these?" The fact itself is, at least as to spiritual things, certainly inadmissible. Conceding that eighty or ninety years ago we had fewer taxes, and many of the articles of life were more cheaply purchasable, how much more than counterbalanced was this by an unconverted ministry, a people perishing for lack of knowledge, a general carelessness with regard to the soul, and an entire unconcern for the enlargement of the Redeemer's kingdom!

At our first interview we could refer to none of the many glorious institutions which are now established. I have not space to enumerate them, nor must I yield myself to enlarge on their claims. But reluctantly to pass by others, one of these has been surpassed by nothing since the days of the apostles; and when I refer to the importance of its design, the simplicity and wisdom of its constitution, the rapidity of its growth, the vastness of its success, the number of languages into which it has translated the Scriptures, and the immensity of copies which it has distributed, I need not say I mean the British and Foreign Bible Society, which may God preserve uninjured, and continue to smile upon, till all shall possess the unsearchable riches of Christ. Since then too, what an extension has there been of evangelical doctrine in the establishment and among the dissenters; and I fearlessly add, of the genuine influences of divine grace in the hearts and lives of thousands! Surely no unprejudiced individual can trace these things, comparatively with what preceded them, and not exclaim, "God hath done great things for us, whereof we are glad."

I rejoice, my dear sir, that a person of your consideration is in the healthful number of those who, notwithstanding the contemptuous denial of some and the gloomy forebodings of others, believe that real religion has been advancing, and is spreading, and will continue to spread, till, without any disruption of the present system, "the earth shall be filled with the knowledge of the Lord as the waters cover the sea: for the mouth of the Lord hath spoken it." [Habakkuk 2:14] You do not expect that a country called by his name, and in which he has such a growing multitude of followers, will be given up of God, and the fountain from which so many streams of health and life are issuing to bless the world will be destroyed. You justly think that the way to gain more is not to despise or disown what the Spirit of God has graciously done for us already; and that the way to improvement is not to run down and condemn every present scheme, attainment, and exertion, because they are not free from those failings which some are too studious to discover, too delighted to expose, and too zealous to enlarge and magnify. If we are not to be weary in well-doing, we need not only exhortation, but hope, which is at once the most active as well as the most cheerful principle. Nothing so unnerves energy and slackens diligence as despondency. Nothing is equally contagious with fear. Those who feel alarm always love to transfuse it. Awful intimations of approaching evils are not only congenial with the melancholic, but the dissatisfied; and while they distress the timid, they charm those who are given to change. It is also easy to perceive that when men have committed themselves in woeful announcements, they immediately feel a kind of prophetical credit at stake, and are under a considerable temptation to welcome disasters as prognostics; for though they may professedly pray against the judgments, they know, and this is a great drawback to their fervency, that their avowed creed requires the calamities as vouchers of the wisdom and truth of their interpretations. If to preserve his reputation from suspicion, after he had cried, Yet forty days and Nineveh shall be destroyed, Jonah himself was sad and sullen, and thought he did well to be angry even unto death, because the city with all the men, women, children, and cattle was not demolished according to his word, what may not be feared from human nature now, if exercised with similar disappointments?

As owing to the mildness and justice of the laws of the paternal government under which we are privileged to live, there is now no outward persecution, and yet, as religion always requires to be tried, we must expect that "from among ourselves will men arise, speaking perverse things to draw away disciples after them;" for "there must be heresies, that they which are of a contrary part may be made manifest." In such cases many are "tossed about by every wind of doctrine," [Ephesians 4:14] till they make "shipwreck of faith and a good conscience." [1 Timothy 1:19] Others, who are not destroyed, suffer loss, especially in the simple, affectionate, devotional frame of their spirit. If good men are injured, they are commonly beguiled: they are drawn aside by some thing piously specious. Any proposal directly erroneous or sinful would excite their alarm as well as aversion. But if the enemy comes transformed into an angel of light, they think they ought not only to receive, but welcome a heavenly visitant: if he enters with the Bible only in his hand, and claims to fix their regards to any thing on that holy ground, they feel themselves not only safe, but even following the will of God; not considering that if, even in the Scriptures, the speculative entices us away from the practical and the mysterious from the plain, and something, though true and good in itself, but subordinate, engrosses the time and attention which should be supremely absorbed by repentance towards God and faith towards our Lord Jesus Christ, his aim may be answered, and "Satan get an advantage over us." Such persons, acting conscientiously, become as determined as martyrs; and continually musing upon one chosen topic, they grow as passionate as lovers, and wonder that all others are not like-minded with them: "The worst of madmen is a saint run mad."

There is not only a pride in dress and beauty, and riches and rank and talent, but of opinion also; a kind of mental vanity, that seeks distinction by peculiarity, and would draw notice by separateness; as that which stands alone is more observable, especially when noise is added to position. In this case the female is easily betrayed beyond some of the decorum of her sex; the younger will not submit to the elder; the hearer sits in judgment on the preacher, and he that is wise in his own conceit will be wiser than seven men that can render a reason. For, "Fools rush in where angels fear to tread."

Mushrooms and less saleable funguses are ordinarily found in a certain kind of rich and rank soil. When religion, from being neglected, becomes all at once the subject of general attention, many will not only be impressed, but surprised and perplexed. The light, good in itself, may for the time be too strong for the weakness of the eye, and the suddenness of the glare may dazzle rather than enlighten. It is very possible for the church, when roused from a state of lethargy, to be in danger from the opposite extreme. The frost of formality may be followed by the fever of enthusiasm.

"Whenever indeed there is a high degree of religious excitement, it cannot be wonderful, considering human ignorance, prejudice, and depravity, that there should be some visionary and strange ebullitions. We have witnessed some of these during the years that are past; but the day in which we now are is singular for the revival—with some perhaps perfectly new pretensions— of most of the notions that were fermented into being at the time of the Commonwealth, and which were then opposed by Owen, Baxter, and others, who had more divinity in their little finger than is to be found in the body, soul, and spirit of many of the modern innovators and improvers, who imagine that their fight is not only "the light of the sun, but the light of seven days!"

A review of history will show that, at the return of less than half a century, some have commonly risen up eager and able to determine the times and the seasons which the Father hath put into his own power and which the apostles were told it was not for them to know. And the same confidence has always been attended with the same success. No gain has ever followed the efforts worthy the time and attention expended upon them; no addition has ever been made to the understanding of the Scriptures; no fresh data have been established from which preachers could safely argue; no practical utility has been afforded to Christians in their private walk with God. And as their documents were not capable of demonstration; as, for want of certainty, they could not become principles of conduct; and as no great impression can belong maintained on the public mind that is not based on obvious truth, the noise of the warfare after a while has always died away, and left us with the conviction that "there is no prophet among us, nor any that telleth how long."

Some prove, in their spiritual genealogy, a descent from Reuben, of whom the dying father said, "Unstable as water, thou shalt not excel." Yet they may strike, and produce a temporary impression in their favor, especially in a country like this—a country proverbial for its credulity, and its more than Athenian rage for something new, whatever be the nature of it. In England: "England, with all thy faults I love thee still—and I can feel, Thy follies too." It has been said by a satirical yet just observer that "any monster will make a man." Who can question this for a moment that has patience to mortify himself as a Briton by reflection and review? Take prodigies. Dwarfs, giants, unnatural births, deformities—the more hideous, the more repelling the spectacles, the more attractive and popular have they always been. Take empiricisms. Their name is Legion; from animal magnetism and the metallic tractors, down to the last infallible remedy for general or specific complaints; all attested and recommended by the most unexceptionable authorities, especially in high life. Take the foals which have been announced for exhibition. Whatever the Promiser has engaged to perform, whether to walk upon the water, or draw himself into a boat He, what large crowds have been drawn together at the time appointed, and with no few of the better sort of people always among them. How has learning been trifled with and degraded! Two or three insulated facts, and a few doubtful or convertible appearances, have been wrought up into a SCIENCE; and some very clever men have advocated its claims to zealous belief, and contrived to puzzle the opponents they could not convince. In the article of preaching, what maneuvers of popularity have not been successfully tried, till there seems hardly any thing left for an experimenter to employ on the folly of the multitude?

But what exemplifications, had we leisure to pursue them, should we find in the article of religious absurdity and extravagance! Has anything been ever broached with confidence that has not gained considerable attention? Did not the effusions of a brother, who died where only he should have lived, in confinement for madness, secure numerous believers and admirers? Had he not defenders from the press? Did he not obtain the notice of a very learned Senator in the House of Commons? And as to the Exeter prophetess; without any one quality to recommend her but ignorance, impudence, and blasphemy, yet did she not make a multitude of converts, not only among the canaille, but among persons of some distinction? And had she not followers and defenders even among the clergy themselves?

All reasoning and all ridicule for the time only served to contribute to the force and obstinacy of the folly. But how just, here, is the remark of an eminent female writer: "Such preposterous pretensions being obviously out of the power of human nature to accomplish, the very extravagance is believed to be supernatural. It is the impossibility which makes the assumed certainty; as the epilepsy of Mahomet confirmed his claims to inspiration." And is there nothing now going forward far exceeding in credulous wonder, arrogant pretension, and miraculous boasting, all that has gone before it, in a country which, in a twofold sense, may well be called "a land of vision?"

One way to become skeptical is, instead of remembering our Lord's words, "If ye know these things, happy are ye if ye do them," [John 13:17] to become critical and curious in religion. A very fruitful source of error is to trample on the distinction of Moses: "The secret things belong unto the Lord our God; but those things which are revealed belong unto us and to our children for ever, that we may do all the words of this law." [Deuteronomy 29:29] The sciences and the arts being human inventions, and therefore not only finite, but imperfect, will allow of new discoveries and every innovation is commonly an improvement, or by experiment it is soon rejected; but we make no scruple to say, that novelty in religion is needless, dangerous, delusive. We are to receive the kingdom of God as a little child. The design of the gospel is to "cast down imaginations and every high thing that exalteth itself against the knowledge of God, and to bring into captivity every thought to the obedience of Christ." [2 Corinthians 10:5]

The maxim often quoted, of a very great and a very good man who blesses and adorns our own age, and who furnishes another proof that first-rate minds are simple and free from eccentricities, "Though we are not to be wise above what is written, we should be wise up to what is written," has been made to justify more than he intended. The apostle considers it a reproach to be "always learning and never able to come to the knowledge of the truth" [2 Timothy 3:7]; and it is a matter of lamentation when persons, perhaps well disposed, are seized with the imagination that there is something of importance to be yet found out in religion, instead of walking in the light, and having the heart established with grace. And what is the subject of these possible or desirable developments? And what lack of motive or of consolation did they feel, who have gone before us in every kind of excellency? And what more perfect characters can we expect than the Leightons and Howes, who, it now seems, were denied illuminations conferred on individuals just entering into the kingdom of God, without a religious education, and from the midst of worldly dissipation or indifference? And where are the superior effects of discoveries, which we are assured not only possess truth, but are of the greatest efficiency? We need not be afraid to compare the converts, the benefactors, the sufferers, the martyrs of one school with those of another. "No man also having drunk old wine, straightway desireth new; for he saith, The old is better."

Here, again, it is refreshing and delightful to turn to one distinguished by consistency, and who has awakened and retained attention so long, not by strangeness, but excellence; not by crying, "Lo here, or Lo there," but by walking steadfastly in the truth; and whose path has not been the glare of the meteor, or the "lawless sweep of the comet," but the shining light of the sun, which shineth more and more unto the perfect day. Nothing would be more satisfactory to the dedicator, now in the evening of life, than to be able lo think, that in this particular he had been in some measure the follower of his admired and honored friend. And by the grace of God, he can say that it has been his aim and prayer to move straight on, never turning aside to the right hand or to the left, to avail himself of any temporary and adventitious aids of popular applause; constantly engaged in pressing only the plain and essential principles of the gospel, and in matters of inferior importance, if not of disputable truth, having faith, to have it to himself before God.

There has been perhaps some little shade of difference in our doctrinal views; but as it has not been sufficient to impair your approbation of my preaching and writings, so I am persuaded you will find nothing in these volumes, should you ever look into them, to offend, even if an occasional reflection does not perfectly suit your own convictions. In one thing it is certain we differ. We are not unwilling respectively to own the Episcopalian and the Dissenter. But in this distinction, we feel conviction without censure, and avow preference without exclusion. And has Providence no concern in such results as these? Suppose, my dear sir, you had been placed originally in my circumstances, and I had been placed in yours; is it impossible or improbable that each of us might have been differently minded from what we now are? Yet who determines the bounds of our habitations? Who administers the events of our birth, and of the days of our earlier and most durable impressions? Who arranges the contacts into which we arc brought with religious connections and spiritual instructors? And does not bigotry, that quarrels with every thing else, arraign the agency of the Most High, and indirectly at least censure him? We do not use this argument without qualification, or push it to every extent; but there are evidently some who not only "judge another man's servant," but another man's Master.

We may in a degree value ourselves as being members of a particular church, but we shall be saved only as members of the church universal; and if we are in a right spirit, we shall prize the name of a Christian a thousand times more than any other name, however extensive or esteemed the religious body from which it is derived.

Uniformity of sentiment may be viewed much in the same way with equality of property. In each case, the thing itself is perfectly impracticable; and if it could be attained it would be injurious, rather than useful. It would abrogate many divine injunctions, contract the sphere of relative virtue, and exclude various duties which go far into the amiableness and perfection of Christian character. It is better to have the protection of the sovereign and the obedience of the subject; the wages of the master, and the labor of the servant; the condescension of the rich and the respect of the poor; the charity of the benefactor, and the gratitude, of the receiver. "If all were the seeing, where were the hearing?" The hands and the feet could not dispense with each other, or even exchange their place and office. If persons acted from hypocrisy, formality, and education only, they might present a kind of sameness; but if they think for themselves, as they are not only allowed, but required to do, it is easy to see, that with the differences there are in the structure of mind, and in outward opportunities and advantages, they cannot fall precisely into the same views. But let them exercise forbearance and candor, let them emulate each other, let the strong bear the infirmities of the weak, and not please themselves, and we shall have a sum of moral excellence far superior to what could be derived from a dull, still, stagnant conformity of opinions. And is it not for this state of things, among those "that hold the head, even Christ that the apostle provides? "Let every one be fully persuaded in his own mind. For one believeth that he may eat all things; another, who is weak, eateth herbs. Let not him that eateth despise him that eateth not; and let not him which eateth not judge him that eateth; for God hath received him. One man esteemeth one day above another; another esteemeth every day alike. Let every man be fully persuaded in his own mind. He that regardeth the day, regardeth it unto the Lord; and he that regardeth not the day, to the Lord he doth not regard it. He that eateth, eateth to the Lord, for he giveth God thanks; and he that eateth not, to the Lord he eateth not, and giveth God thanks. For none of us liveth to himself, and no man dieth to himself. For whether we live, we live unto the Lord; and whether we die, we die unto the Lord ; whether we live therefore, or die, we are the Lord's. But why dost thou judge thy brother? or why dost thou set at naught thy brother? For we shall all stand before the judgment seat of Christ. For it is written, "As I live, saith the Lord, every knee shall bow to me, and every tongue shall confess to God. So then every one of us shall give account of himself to God." [Romans 14:5-12] The quotation is long; but I fear the principles of the reasoning and the enforcements are not as yet duly regarded by any religious party; though there are, in our respective communities, individuals who walk by the same rule, and mind the same thing. And I cannot forbear adding a few more of those fine texts which do not exclude the number, but diminish the importance of the articles of difference, and press only those in which Christians agree: "The kingdom of God is not meat and drink; but righteousness, and peace, and joy in the Holy Ghost." [Romans 14:17] "We are the circumcision which worship God in the spirit, and rejoice in Christ Jesus, and have no confidence in the flesh." [Philippians 3:3] "In Christ Jesus neither circumcision availeth any thing, nor uncircumcision, but a new creature." [Galatians 6:15] "In Jesus Christ neither circumcision availeth any thing, nor uncircumcision; but faith which worketh by love." [Galatians 5:6] Let us abide in the liberty wherewith Christ has made us free. [Galatians 5:1] He has set our feet in a large place. There is room enough in the plain around Stonehenge for persons to walk and commune together very commodiously; why should they try to get on some old mole hills, or barrows over the dead, or hedge-banks, where they must press against each other, or jostle each other down?

A cordial agreement in the essentials of the gospel should induce us to put up with minor differences; and a superior and constant engagement of the soul to the most important objects of religion will draw off, comparatively, the attention from inferior ones, leaving us neither leisure nor relish for them.

When, therefore, in reference to the latter day glory, it is said, "They shall see eye to eye," we are persuaded, with Baxter, that there may not be a much more complete uniformity of opinion in many things than there now is. But there will be a more perfect accordance in great things, and a more perfect agreement concerning lesser ones. They will see eye to eye as to the propriety of one measure: that if we cannot be of one mind, we should, like the first converts at Jerusalem, be "of one heart and of one soul."

But does not the Scripture speak much of unity among Christians? It does; and what that oneness is, may be inferred from fact as well as from reasoning. The Saviour prayed that "all" His followers might be "one;" and God had before promised that He would give His people "one heart and one way." Now it can hardly be supposed that this prayer and this promise have not been accomplished. But if they have been fulfilled, it has not been in a sameness of sentiment with regard to a number of things pertaining to religion, but with regard to the substance of religion itself: a oneness unaffected by minuter distinctions—a oneness which included as servants of the same Lord, and as guests at the same table, a Hopkins and a Bates, a Watts and a Newton, a Porteus and a Hall—a oneness that resembles the identity of human nature, notwithstanding all the varieties of man.

When will some persons believe or remember that where there are no parts, there can be no union; that where there is no variety, there can be no harmony; that it doth not follow because one thing is right that another is absolutely wrong; that others differ no further from us than we differ from others; that it is meanness and injustice to assume a freedom we refuse to yield; that children differing in age and size and dress and schooling and designation belong to the same family; and that the grain growing in various fields and distances is wheat still, sown by the same hand, and to lie gathered into the same garner?

And would it not be well for us often to reflect on the state of things in another world, where it is believed by all, that the differences which now too often keep the true disciples of Christ at a distance from each other will be done away? And to ask ourselves whether we are not likely to be the more complete, the more we resemble the spirits of just men made perfect? And whether we must not have a meetness for glory, before we can enjoy it? But what preparation in kind, what in degree, for such a communion above, have they who feel only aversion to all those who, however holy and heavenly, walk not with them in the outward order of religious administrations? How special and circumscribed is what some mean by the communion of saints! It only respects those within their own inclosures. They would inhibit their members from having much intercourse in company, and from all, even occasional intermixture in religious exercises, with those they hope to mingle with forever! But not to observe that such intercourse and intermixture are perfectly consistent with general and avowed regularity of preference and practice, and the good influence it has to remove the haughty and offensive repulsion of exclusiveness, is there— as "we are taught of God to love one another," [1 John 4:7] and as "every one that loveth him that begat, loveth him also that is begotten of him" [1 John 5:1]— is there no danger of putting a force upon pious tendencies, and of chilling the warmth of holy emotions by the coldness and abstraction of system and rules? The remark of Paley on another subject may be well applied here. He is arguing the propriety of refusing every application of common beggars for relief. Some, he observes, have recommended the practice by strong reasonings; and he himself seems much inclined to the same side. But he is too frank not to ask, "Yet, after all, is it not to be feared lest such invariable refusing should suffocate benevolent feeling?"

You, my dear sir, are a proof that Christian liberality may abound without laxity and without inconsistency. And other instances of the same lovely character are increasingly coming forward, in which we see how rigid contention for minor partialities can yield to the force of Christian charity, and disappear before the grandeur of "the common salvation," and the grace of "one God and Father of all, who is above all, and through all, and in us all." "Perhaps," says Robert Hall, "there never was so much unanimity witnessed among the professors of serious piety as at the present. Systems of religion fundamentally erroneous are falling into decay, while the subordinate points of difference, which do not affect the principal verities of Christianity, nor the ground of hope, are either consigned to oblivion, or are the subjects of temperate and amicable controversy; and in consequence of their subsiding to their just level, the former appear in their great and natural magnitude. And if the religion of Christ ever assumes her ancient lusters—and we are assured by the highest authority she will— it must be by retracing our steps, by reverting to the original principles on which, as a social institution, it was founded: we must go back to the simplicity of the first ages; we must learn to quit a subtle and disputatious theology, for a religion of love emanating from a few divinely energetic principles which pervade every page of inspiration, and demand nothing for their adoption and belief besides a humble and contrite heart."

Bunyan, in his *Holy War*, says that Mr. Prejudice fell down and broke his leg: "I wish," adds the honest—and Mr. Southey himself does not refuse him the attribute—the matchless allegorist, "he had broken his neck." Cordially joining in this devout wish, and apologizing for the undesigned length and freedom of this desultory address, allow me, with every sentiment of regard and esteem, to subscribe myself,

My dear Sir, Your much obliged and humble friend and servant,
William Jay

Evening Exercises for Every Day in the Year
By Rev. William Jay
American Tract Society
1865

Chapter Twelve

TRIBUTE TO WILLIAM WILBERFORCE ON THE PLAQUE IN WESTMINSTER ABBEY WHERE HE IS BURIED

In an age and country fertile in great and good men,

He was among the foremost of those who fixed the character of our times because to high and various talents, to warm benevolence, and to universal candour.

He added the abiding eloquence of the Christian life.

Eminent as he was in every department of public labour

And a leader in every work of charity.

Whether to relive the temporal or the spiritual wants of his fellow men

His name will ever be specially identified with those exertions

Which, by the blessing of God, removed from England

The guilt of the African slave trade, and prepared the way for the Abolition of Slavery in every colony of the Empire.

THE ABOLITION OF SLAVERY
AND "THE BETTER HOUR"

William Wilberforce and the Clapham Group

In *The Tale of Two Cities*, Charles Dickens writing about the late 1780s in England and France described it as "the best of times and the worst of times." For the wealthy, life was very good. The evening entertainment in the clubs in England included the theater, gambling and women. Servants for the wealthy were plentiful. Yet, on the other hand, times for others were tough. The Industrial Revolution had just begun. Children were in enforced labor, often working 15 to 16 hour days in unsafe conditions. Some worked in the new textile mills. Others worked as chimney sweeps. Only 25 percent of children made it to adulthood. For stealing a scarf, children were executed. Public hanging was a public entertainment of the day for which people paid money to get the best seats. The biggest evil of the day, that of slavery in the plantations of the West Indies, was the unseen evil. Eleven million human beings had been captured and taken from Africa to the West Indies to work in slavery and bondage. Britain had the biggest portion of the slave trade. Many of the human beings were thrown overboard alive so that ship owners could collect insurance.

Enter several of the prominent wealthy men and women that saw all of these conditions as wrong and gave of their time, their talent and their money to change the world around them. A young English Member of Parliament, William Wilberforce, writing on Sunday, October 28, 1787, wrote in his journal: "God Almighty has set before me two great objects, the suppression of the slave trade and the reformation manners."

Wilberforce pursued both objectives with vigor and persistence despite opposition and vilification that was overwhelming at times and costly to his health. After 20 years of struggle, Wilberforce and his colleagues that lived in the Clapham area 5 miles south of the center of London were able to achieve legislation in England regarding the abolition of the slave trade and to have greatly influenced the abolition of the slave trade in America and ultimately in France, as well. In another 26 years, just as he died on July 29, 1833, Wilberforce was informed that Parliament had agreed to the emancipation of slavery.

Wilberforce and his Clapham colleagues, including Granville Sharp, John Thornton, Henry Thornton, Thomas Clarkson, Hannah More and others, each played a part based on their own skills. Granville Sharp, as a lawyer, provided legal guidance. The Thortons provided money and a popular place to meet. Clarkson rode tirelessly on his horse around England, collecting research on slavery by going on board as many of the slave ships as possible and poring through records. Hannah More brought to bear her popularity as a prominent playwright. Together, they changed the world in a number of ways:

First, slavery had been a way of life every since the early civilizations of Egypt, Greece, Israel and Rome. It had continued through the Middle Ages with serfs. While people may have found it distasteful at times, there was never an organized movement to abolish it until the late 18th century. After studying the situation of slavery, particularly the "Middle Passage," Wilberforce jumped into action. "So enormous, so dreadful, so irremediable did the Trade's wickedness appear," Wilberforce told Parliament, "that my own mind was completely made up for Abolition. Let the consequences be what they would, I from this time determined that I would never rest until I had effected its abolition."

Second, Wilberforce who spearheaded the effort in Parliament through his friendships among others with close friend William Pitt the Younger, the Prime Minister, invented issue-campaigning along the way. Today, when people get involved in promoting issues, such as cancer research through Lance Armstrong's familiar yellow bracelet, they are drawing upon the pioneering work that Wilberforce did in getting Josiah Wedgwood to design a medallion of a black slave in chains on his knees with the inscription: "Am I not a man and a brother?" This medallion was put on plates and used as dinner launchers to bring out a discussion of black slaves, few of whom had ever seen in person in England, but all who had owned land in the West Indies, including many Members of Parliament, had benefited from financially. With the backdrop of the French Revolution in 1789 and the Reign of Terror in which thousands were sent to the guillotine, including the King and Queen, Wilberforce and his friends organized massive petitions from the people of England. This was an incredibly risky undertaking, given the nervousness of the establishment. One of the many petitions contained over 800,000 signatures, approximately 10 percent of the population in England and was rolled down the floor of Parliament while it was in session. This would be equivalent of collecting 28 million signatures in America and rolling the signatures down the House and the Senate in Congress. Wilberforce and his friends were incredibly effective in bringing issues of the times to the fore.

Third, Wilberforce and his friends pioneered in the field of philanthropy. Wilberforce either started or participated in sixty-nine charities. He created the Society for the Prevention of Cruelty to Animals, which was a huge issue of the day. He also started the Society for the Betterment of the Poor and was a founder of the British and Foreign Bible Society, now the Bible Society, and many other charities, as well.

Wilberforce also made a point with his philanthropy. In one instance, he paid for African children to come to England and be educated so that he could demonstrate that Africans were as bright as other human beings. Wilberforce and his friends had a compassion for the oppressed and poor that was turned into action over a broad range of issues, although the abolition of slavery was always first and foremost. Yet, much of the money that was given was done so anonymously, as Wilberforce sought no credit.

Fourth, Wilberforce did this out of the "great change" he experienced in coming face to face with a deeper Christianity that he experienced in 1784, as he traveled in Europe with a former tutor, Isaac Milner. The old Wilberforce who had been the "pit bull" of Prime Minister William Pitt and who viciously attacked the opposition became the kind, but firm leader who worked with everyone possible and became greatly admired by all, even the opposition. Wilberforce was even able to work with the likes of Charles Fox, who he had previously attacked. To mark his change and to encourage others to do so, Wilberforce with so many other tasks and responsibilities as a Member of Parliament wrote *A Practical View of Christianity* which became a best seller for fifty years and ultimately became a true classic, the first religious book other than the Bible to do so at the time. William Cowper, the British poet, in a tribute to Wilberforce in a sonnet, described Wilberforce as bringing "the better hour."

William Wilberforce is an unsung hero of the humanities and a giant in his own time. While virtually unknown in the United States today, Wilberforce was acknowledged by Abraham Lincoln in 1856 as a person that "every school boy" in America knew. The emancipation leader Frederick Douglass saluted the energy of Wilberforce and his co-workers "that finally thawed the British heart into sympathy for the slave, and moved the strong arm of government in mercy to put an end to this bondage. Let no American, especially no colored American, withhold generous recognition of this stupendous achievement—a triumph of right over wrong, of good over evil, and a victory for the whole human race."

Chapter Thirteen

WILBERFORCE'S TEXT

By F. W. Boreham

The hand that struck the shackles from the galled limbs of our British slaves was the hand of a hunchback. One of the triumphs of statuary in Westminster Abbey is the seated figure that, whilst faithfully perpetuating the noble face and fine features of Wilberforce, skillfully conceals his frightful physical deformities. From infancy he was an elfish, misshapen little figure. At the Grammar School at Hull, the other boys would lift his tiny, twisted form on to the table and make him go through all his impish tricks. For, though so pitifully stunted and distorted, he was amazingly sprightly, resourceful and clever. A master of mimicry, a born actor, an accomplished singer and a perfect elocutionist, he was as agile, also, as a monkey and as full of mischief. Every day he enlivened his performance by the startling introduction of some fresh antics that convulsed alike his schoolfellows and his teachers. He is the most striking illustration that history can offer of a grotesque and insignificant form glorified by its consecration to a great and noble cause.

Recognizing the terrible handicap that Nature had imposed upon him, he set himself to counterbalance matters by acquiring a singular graciousness and charm of manner. He succeeded so perfectly that his courtliness and grace became proverbial. It was said of him that, if you saw him in conversation with a man, you would suppose that the man was his brother, or, if with a woman, that he was her lover. He made men forget his strange appearance. When he sprang to his feet to plead the cause of the slave, he seemed like a man inspired, and his disfigurement magically vanished. "I saw," says Boswell, in his letter to Mr. Dundas, "I saw a shrimp mount the table; but, as I listened, he grew and grew until the shrimp became a whale!" When he rose to address the House of Commons, he looked like a dwarf that had jumped out of a fairy-tale; when he resumed his seat, he looked like the giant of the self-same story.

His form, as the *Times* said, "was like the letter S; it resembled a stick that could not be straightened." Yet his hearers declare that his face, when pleading for the slave, was like the face of an angel. The ugliness of his little frame seemed to disappear; and, under the magic of his passionate eloquence, his form became sublime.

When, in 1833, he passed away, such a funeral procession made its way to Westminster Abbey as even London had rarely witnessed. He was borne to his last resting place by the Peers and Commoners of England with the Lord Chancellor at their head.

In imperishable marble it was recorded of him that "He had removed from England the guilt of the slave-trade and prepared the way for the abolition of slavery in every colony in the Empire." And it is said that, as the cortege made its sombre way through the crowded streets, all London was in tears, and one person in every four was garbed in deepest black.

II

Among Sir James Stephen's masterpieces of biological analysis, there is nothing finer than his essay on Wilberforce. But he confesses to a difficulty. "There is," he says, "something hidden. You cannot account for his stupendous influence by pointing to anything that lies upon the surface. What that hidden life really was," Sir James observes, "none but himself could know, and few indeed could even plausibly conjecture. But even they who are the least able to solve the enigma may acknowledge and feel that there was some secret spring of action on which his strength was altogether dependent." Now, what was that hidden factor ? What was the "secret spring of action" that explains this strangely handicapped yet wonderfully useful life? Can I lay my finger on the source of all these beneficent energies? Can I trace the hidden power that impelled and directed these fruitful and epoch-making activities? I think I can. Behind all that appears upon the surface there lies a great experience, a great thought, a great text. I find it at the beginning of his career; I find it again at the close.

As a youth, preparing himself to play some worthy part in life, Wilberforce travels. Thrice he tours Europe, once in the company of William Pitt, then a young fellow of exactly his own age, and twice in the company of Isaac Milner, the brilliant brother of his Hull schoolmaster. It was in the course of one of these tours that the crisis of his inner life overtook him. Milner and he made it a practice to carry with them a few books to read on rainy days. Among these oddly assorted volumes they slipped into their luggage a copy of Dr. Doddridge's *Rise and Progress of Religion in the Soul.* It was a dangerous companion for young men who prized their peace of mind; no book of that period had provoked more serious thought. It certainly set Wilberforce thinking; and not all the festivities of his tour, nor the laughter of his friends could dispel the feeling that now took sole possession of his mind. One over-powering emotion drove out all others. It haunted him sleeping and waking. "My sin!" he cried, "my sin, my sin, my sin!"—it was this thought of his condition that filled him with apprehension and despair.

"The deep guilt and black ingratitude of my past life," he says, "forced itself upon me in the strongest colors; and I condemned myself for having wasted my precious time and talents. It was not so much the fear of punishment as a sense of my great sinfulness. Such was the effect which this thought produced that for months I was in a state of the deepest depression from strong conviction of my guilt!"

"My deep guilt!"

"My great sinfulness!"

"My black ingratitude!"

It was then, at the age of twenty-six, that his soul gathered itself up in one great and bitter cry: "God, be merciful to me a sinner!" he implored; and, on receiving an assurance that his prayer was heard—as all such prayers must be—he breaks out in a new strain: "What infinite love," he says, "that Christ should die to save such a sinner!"

"My sin! My sin! My sin!"

"God, be merciful to me a sinner!"

"That Christ should die to save such a sinner!"

This was in 1785. Wilberforce stood then at the dawn of his great day.

For the second scene we must pass over nearly half a century. His career is drawing to its close. The twisted little body is heavily swathed in wrappings and writhes in pain. Hearing of his serious sickness, his Quaker friend, Mr. Joseph Gurney, comes to see him.

"He received me with the warmest marks of affection," Mr. Gurney says, "and seemed delighted at the unexpected arrival of an old friend. The illuminated expression of his furrowed countenance, with his clasped and uplifted hands,were indicative of profound devotion and holy joy. He unfolded his experience to me in a highly interesting manner."

"With regard to myself," said Mr. Wilberforce, before taking a last farewell of his friend, "with regard to myself, I have nothing whatever to urge but the poor publican's plea, 'God be merciful to me a sinner!'"

"These words," adds Mr. Gurney, "were expressed with peculiar feeling and emphasis."

"God, be merciful to me a sinner!"—it was the cry of his heart in 1785, as his life lay all before him.

"God, be merciful to me a sinner!"—it was still the cry of his heart in 1833, as his life lay all behind.

Here, then, is William Wilberforce's text! It will do us good to listen to it as, once and again, it falls from his lips. In outlining the events that led Christiana to forsake the City of Destruction and to follow her husband on his pilgrimage, Bunyan tells us that she had a dream, "And behold, in her dream, she saw as if a broad parchment was opened before her, in which was recorded the sum of her ways; and the times, as she thought, looked very black upon her. Then she cried out aloud in her sleep, 'God, be merciful to me a sinner!' And the little children heard her." It was well that she cried: it was well that the children heard: it led to their setting out together for the Cross, the Palace Beautiful and the City of Light. It will be well indeed for us if, listening to William Wilberforce as he offers the same agonizing petition, we, like Christiana's children, become followers of his faith and sharers of his joy.

III

They are very few, I suppose, who would envy William Wilberforce the wretchedness that darkened his soul at Spa in the course of that third European tour, the wretchedness that led him to cry out for the everlasting mercy. He was then twenty-six; and if any young fellow of twenty-six entertains the slightest doubt as to the desirability of such a mournful experience, I should like to introduce that young fellow first to Robinson Crusoe and then to old William Cottee of Theydon Bois. We all remember the scene in which Robinson Crusoe, soon after his shipwreck, searched the old chest for tobacco and found—a Bible! He began to read.

"It was not long after I set seriously to this work," he tells us, "that I found my heart more deeply and sincerely affected with the wickedness of my past life. The impression of my dream revived, and the words, 'All these things have not brought thee to repentance,' ran seriously in my thoughts. I was earnestly begging of God to give me repentance, when it happened providentially, that very day, that, reading the Scripture, I came to these words, 'He is exalted a Prince and a Saviour to give repentance and to give remission.' I threw down the book, and, with my heart as well as my hands lifted up in Heaven, in a kind of ecstasy of joy, I cried out aloud, 'Jesus, Thou Son of David, Thou exalted Prince and Saviour, give me repentance.' This was the first time that I could say, in the true sense of the word, that I prayed in all my life!"

"Give me repentance!"—this was Robinson Crusoe's first prayer. But, for William Wilberforce, bemoaning at Spa the list of his transgressions, the prayer is already answered. They may pity him who will; Robinson Crusoe will offer him nothing but congratulations.

So will old William Cottee. The old gentleman was well over ninety, and was bedridden, when, in my college days, I visited him. He has long since passed from his frailty to his felicity. I used occasionally to preach in the village sanctuary, and was more than once the guest of the household that he adorned. No such visit was complete without an invitation to go upstairs and have a talk with grandfather. As a rule, however, those talks with grandfather were a little embarrassing to a mere student, for a ministerial student moves in an atmosphere in which his theological opinions are treated, to say the least, with respect. He is quite sure of them himself, and he likes other people to exhibit equal confidence. But poor old William Cottee had no respect at all for any theological opinions of mine. He was a sturdy old hyper-Calvinist, and, to him, the doctrines that I expounded with such assurance were mere milk and water—mostly water.

One afternoon I found the old gentleman bewailing the exceeding sinfulness of his evil heart. This seemed to me, viewing the matter from the point of view of a theological student, a very primitive experience for so mature a saint. Perhaps I as good as said so; I forget. I only remember that, in response to my shallow observation, the old gentleman sat straight up in bed—a thing I had never seen him do before—stared at me with eyes so full of reproach that they seemed to pierce my very soul, and slowly recited a verse that I had never before heard and have never since forgotten:

What comfort can a Saviour bring
To those who never felt their woe?

A sinner is a sacred thing
The Holy Ghost hath made him so!

Ministers often learn from those they seem to teach; but
it rarely happens that a profound and awful and searching
truth rushes as startlingly upon a man as this one did that
day upon me. It is a hard saying; who can hear it? But the
wise will understand. Because of the lesson that he then taught
me—to say nothing of the fact that one of his granddaughters
has proved for many years the best wife any minister ever
had—I have always thought kindly of old William Cottee. I
never heard the old man refer to Robinson Crusoe in any
way; but I am sure that he would join the redoubtable islander
in congratulating William Wilberforce on the experience that
overtook him in his twenty-sixth year. The sunlit passages in
life are not always the most profitable: it is through much
tribulation that we enter the kingdom.

IV

"My sin! My sin! My sin!"
"God, be merciful to me a sinner!"
"What infinite love that Christ should die to save such a
sinner!"
Wilberforce felt that such infinite love demanded the
fullest requital he could possibly offer. Those who have been
greatly saved must greatly serve. I like to think of that
memorable day on which the two friends—Wilberforce and
Pitt—lay sprawling on the grass under a grand old oak tree
in the beautiful park at Hoi Wood, in Kent. A solid stone
seat now stands beside the tree, bearing an inscription
commemorative of the historic occasion. For it was then—
and there—that Wilberforce solemnly devoted his life to the
emancipation of the slaves. He had introduced the subject

with some diffidence; was delighted at Pitt's evident sympathy; and, springing to his feet, he declared that he would set to work at once to abolish the iniquitous traffic. Few of us realize the immense proportions that the British slave trade had then assumed. During the eighteenth century, nearly a million blacks were transported, with much less consideration than would have been shown to cattle, from Africa to Jamaica alone. From his earliest infancy, the horror of the traffic preyed upon the sensitive mind of William Wilberforce. When quite a boy he wrote to the papers, protesting against "this odious traffic in human flesh." Now, a young fellow in the twenties, he made its extinction the purpose of his life. For fifty years he never rested. Through evil report and through good, he tirelessly pursued his ideal. At times the opposition seemed insuperable. But Pitt stood by him; the Quakers and a few others encouraged him to persist; John Wesley, only a few days before his death, wrote begging the reformer never to give up. After twenty years of incessant struggle, it was enacted that the exportation of slaves from Africa should cease; but no relief was offered to those already in bondage. A quarter of a century later, as Wilberforce lay dying, messengers from Westminster entered his room to tell him that at last, at last, the Emancipation Bill had been passed; the slaves were free! "Thank God!" exclaimed the dying man, "thank God that I have lived to see this day!" Like Wolfe at Quebec, like Nelson at Trafalgar, like Sir John Franklin in the Northwest Passage, he died in the flush of triumph. He had resolved that, as an expression of his gratitude for his own deliverance, he would secure for the slaves their freedom; and he passed away rejoicing that their fetters were all broken and gone.

V

"God, be merciful to me a sinner!"—this was his prayer in 1785, as his life lay all before him.

"God be merciful to me a sinner!"—this was his prayer in 1833, as he lay dying, his life's work accomplished.

William Wilberforce reminds me of William MacLure. There were many saints in Drumtochty, but there was no greater saint than old Dr. MacLure. Rich and poor, young and old—the good doctor on his white pony had fought his way through the dark nights and the deep snowdrifts of the glen to help and heal them all. And now he is dying himself! Drumsheugh sits beside the bed. The doctor asks him to read a bit. Drumsheugh puts on his spectacles.

"Ma mither," he says, "aye wanted this read tae her when she was sairly sick, and he begins to read, 'In My Father's house are many mansions ...'" But the doctor stops him.

"It's a bonnie word," he says, "but it's no for the likes o' me!" And he makes him read the parable of the Pharisee and the Publican till he comes to the words, "God, be merciful to me a sinner!"

"That micht hae been written for me, Drumsheugh, or any ither auld sinner that has feenished his life, an' he's naething tae say for himself."

Exactly so spoke William Wilberforce. Mr. Gurney quoted many great and comfortable Scriptures, but the dying man shook his head.

"With regard to myself," he said, "I have nothing whatever to urge but the poor publican's plea, 'God, be merciful to me a sinner!'"

In what better company than in the company of William MacLure and William Wilberforce can we enter the Kingdom of God?

BIBLIOGRAPHY

1. Hancock, Christopher. The "Shrimp" who Stopped Slavery, *Christian History*, Issue 53 (Vol. XVI, No. 1)
2. The New Schaff-Herzog Religious Encyclopedia, Volumn XII. *William Wilberforce*
3. Enoch, E. E. Twelve Marvelous Men. Schmul Publishing Co., Inc. Salem, Ohio
4. Fendall, Lon. *William Wilberforce: Abolitionist, Politician, Writer.* Barbour Books. 2002
5. Lean, Garth. *God's Politician.* Helmers & Howard, Colorado Springs. 1987
6. Jay, Rev. William. *Evening Exercises for Every Day in the Year.* American Tract Society
7. Boreham, F. W. *A Bunch of Everlastings.* Judson Press. 1920
8. Lamartine, Hazlitt. *Spirit of the Age or Contemporary Portraits.* Wiley and Putnam, New York. 1846
9. Curtis, Ken. Glimpses issue #87 from Christian History Institute. (www.chinstitute.org)

INDEX

A

A Serious Call to a Devout and Holy Life 8

abolition 10, 11, 12, 13, 14, 16, 19, 21, 22, 25, 30, 35, 36, 132, 148, 171, 173, 176

of slavery 13, 22, 30, 35

abolitionist 11, 20

Abolitionist Movement 11

Africa 15, 16, 20, 26, 29

African Institution 20

Age of Reason 22

Amazing Grace 9, 32, 34

America 15, 26, 36

Anti-Slavery Society 20, 21

Appeal on Behalf of the Negro Slaves 20

Appeal to the Religion, Justice and Humanity of the Inhabitants of the British Empire 21, 25

Archbishop of Canterbury 136, 137

B

Barbauld, Anna Laetitia xii

Boswell, James 2, 36

Bunyan, John 168, 179

Buxton, Thomas Fowell 12, 13, 21

C

Christian character 100, 120, 163

Christian Observer 132

Christianity viii, xiii, xiv, 1, 8, 9, 20, 23, 24, 26, 35, 36, 37, 43, 44, 45, 46, 48, 49, 53, 54, 56, 57, 58, 71, 73, 82, 84, 98, 103, 104, 105, 107, 110, 115, 117, 118, 119, 120, 121, 122, 147, 153, 167, 173

Christians, nominal viii, 44, 53, 63, 79, 99, 101, 117

Church of England 76, 107

Clapham Group 31, 33, 38

Clapham Sect 21, 23, 33, 35

Claphamites 33, 35, 39

Clarkson, Thomas 11, 14, 18, 25

Constitution of the United States 132

Cowper, William 19

Crusoe, Robinson 180, 181, 182

D

Dickens, Charles 170

Doddridge, Philip 8, 26, 34

Douglass, Frederick 173

E

emancipation 20, 21, 25, 36, 133, 171, 173, 182, 183

Emancipation Proclamation vii

evangelicalism 8, 23, 25

F

faith xv, 8, 9, 24, 25, 36, 45, 49, 50, 75, 76, 100, 102, 107, 108, 111, 113, 115, 120, 156, 157, 162, 165, 179

Christian 24

freedom 13, 22, 43, 128, 148, 151, 166, 168, 183

French Revolution 15

G

Gisbourne, Thomas 38

Gospel vii, viii, 23, 37, 46, 48, 57, 78, 80, 102, 105, 106, 108, 109, 161, 162, 165

social 23

grace 2, 73, 75, 76, 85, 86, 97, 100, 103, 104, 106, 107, 113, 120, 152, 155, 161, 162, 167, 175

Grant, Charles 34, 38

guilt 47, 51, 69, 74, 108, 169, 176, 178

H

Holy Spirit 75, 76, 80, 97, 99, 101, 105, 108, 116, 121

House of Commons 7, 9, 11, 12, 13, 21

House of Lords 12

humility 116, 120

J

Jesus vii, 46, 49, 58, 75, 77, 81, 88, 94, 98, 100, 103, 107, 108, 109, 111, 113, 122, 152, 157, 164, 180

Johnson, Ben 138

justice 58, 70, 71, 73, 93, 103, 105, 120, 132, 156

K

King George III 5, 22

Kingdom of Christ 49

L

Law, William 8

love 3, 37, 55, 76, 77, 79, 81,
85, 86, 88, 93, 95, 98, 99,
106, 111, 116, 117, 120,
127, 165, 168, 178, 182

of Christ 79, 81, 99, 111

lukewarmness 85

M

Macaulay, Zachary 34, 35,
36, 38

manners 10, 22, 24, 128, 134,
170

reformation of 10, 22, 24

mercy 2, 74, 75, 96, 102,
104, 105, 106, 110, 147,
152, 174, 180

Methodism 3, 17

Methodist 9

missions 38

morality vii, 22, 44, 109

morals vii, 10, 14, 22, 35, 46,
48, 56, 120, 128

More, Hannah 23, 31, 34, 35,
38, 171

N

Nelson, Horatio 16, 18

New York Daily Advocate
131

Newton, John xiii, 9, 10, 17,
19, 32, 34, 62, 153, 166

O

opium 2

P

paganism 119

Paine, Thomas 22

Parliament 131, 132, 133,
135, 138, 170, 171, 172,
173

Pitt, William 2, 4, 6, 9, 10,
13, 16, 31, 32, 34, 137,
172, 173, 177, 182

pride 54, 55, 67, 69, 81, 117,
118, 120, 121, 147, 157

of human nature 54, 67

Providence 10, 46, 48, 82,
162

Q

Quakers 183

R

Redeemer 37, 95, 98, 106,
108, 111, 120

repentance 65, 75, 100, 111, 113, 157, 180

reprobate mind 56

Rise and Progress of Religion in the Soul 8, 26, 34

S

Savior 49, 72, 75, 76, 83, 93, 94, 95, 97, 99, 101, 102, 103, 106, 107, 109, 110, 111

shame vii, xii, 56, 94, 125, 129

Sharp, Granville 11, 34, 36, 38

Shore, John 34

Sierra Leone 20, 35

slavery 1, 10, 11, 12, 14, 15, 17, 20, 21, 22, 25, 26, 29, 30, 32, 33, 34, 35, 38

Smith, Sir William 38

Society for the Abolition of the Slave Trade 11

Society for the Mitigation and Gradual Abolition 13, 21

Society for the Suppression of Vice 22

Society of Friends 11

Spooner, Barbara 7

Stephen, James 34, 38

T

Teignmouth, Lord 38

Thornton, Henry 21

Thornton, Henry 34, 35, 38

Thornton, John 171

Thoughts on the Manners of the Great 23

U

Unitarians 78

V

Venn, John 39

virtue 22, 24, 44, 54, 57, 58, 117, 119, 120, 127, 145, 148, 163

W

Wesley, Charles 23

Wesley, John 14, 17, 18

West Indies 15, 20, 21, 25, 29

Westminster Abbey 22, 26, 31

Whitefield, George 3

wisdom 71, 73, 81, 83, 84, 92, 93, 107, 112, 116, 120, 153, 154, 156